MASTERING BIG DATA ANALYTICS: TOOLS TECHNIQUES AND BEST PRACTICES

DR.G.MANIMALA

Made with ♥ on the Notion Press Platform
www.notionpress.com

Contents

CHAPTER ONE

INTRODUCTION

Big data analytics is the process of examining large volumes of data to uncover hidden patterns, correlations, and other useful information that can be used to make informed business decisions. It involves a complex interplay of technologies, tools, and human expertise.

In today's data-driven world, organizations are inundated with vast amounts of information from diverse sources. The ability to harness this data and extract meaningful insights is no longer a luxury but a necessity for survival and growth. Big data analytics empowers businesses to make data-driven decisions, optimize operations, and gain a competitive edge.

This book is your comprehensive guide to mastering the art and science of big data analytics. We delve into the core concepts, tools, techniques, and best practices that form the foundation of successful data-driven initiatives. Whether you're a seasoned data scientist, a business analyst seeking to expand your skill set, or a curious enthusiast, this book will equip you with the knowledge and skills to unlock the full potential of your data.

Join us as we explore the exciting world of big data analytics, from understanding the fundamentals to implementing advanced analytics techniques. Together, we will uncover the hidden value within your data and transform it into a powerful asset for your organization.

Key Topics Covered

- **Understanding Big Data:** Exploring the characteristics and challenges of big data.
- **Data Preparation and Management:** Cleaning, transforming, and preparing data for analysis.
- **Data Exploration and Visualization:** Discovering insights through visual exploration.
- **Statistical Analysis:** Applying statistical methods to uncover patterns and relationships.
- **Machine Learning and Predictive Modeling:** Building predictive models to forecast future trends.
- **Big Data Tools and Technologies:** Leveraging popular tools and platforms for big data processing.
- **Real-World Applications:** Exploring case studies and industry-specific use cases.
- **Ethical Considerations:** Addressing privacy, bias, and security concerns.

By the end of this book, you will be well-equipped to tackle complex data challenges, extract valuable insights, and drive data-driven decision-making within your organization.

CHAPTER TWO

BIG DATA PHENOMENON

The digital revolution has ushered in an era of unprecedented data generation. From social media interactions to online transactions, every aspect of modern life leaves a digital footprint.

This exponential growth of data, often referred to as Big Data, has transformed the way businesses operate, governments make decisions, and individuals interact with the world.

Key Characteristics of Big Data

- **Volume:** The sheer quantity of data generated is immense. Petabytes and exabytes of data are now commonplace.
- **Velocity:** Data is generated and processed at incredible speeds, requiring real-time analysis capabilities.
- **Variety:** Data comes in diverse formats, including structured, unstructured, and semi-structured data.
- **Veracity:** Data quality and accuracy can vary significantly, impacting the reliability of insights.
- **Value:** Extracting meaningful insights from Big Data is crucial for driving business value and innovation.

The Impact of Big Data

- **Business Transformation:** Big Data enables organizations to make data-driven decisions, optimize operations, and identify new market opportunities.

Big data analytics is the catalyst for profound business transformation. By harnessing the vast amounts of data generated daily, organizations can make informed decisions, optimize operations, and uncover hidden opportunities.

Key areas where big data drives transformation:

Data-Driven Decision Making:

- Data-driven decision making (DDDM) is a strategic approach that involves using facts, metrics, and data to inform business decisions.
- It's a shift from relying on intuition or past experiences (gut feelings) to making choices based on concrete evidence.

Why is Data-Driven Decision Making Important?

- **Increased accuracy:** Data provides a clear picture of the situation, reducing the risk of making incorrect decisions.
- **Improved efficiency**: By understanding what works and what doesn't, businesses can optimize processes and resource allocation.
- **Enhanced competitiveness**: Data-driven companies are often more agile and responsive to market changes.
- **Better decision justification**: Data-backed decisions are easier to explain and defend.

Data-Driven Decision Making Process:

- **Define the Problem**: Clearly articulate the business question or challenge you want to address.
- **Data Collection**: Gather relevant data from various sources, ensuring it's accurate and complete.
- **Data Analysis**: Use statistical methods and data visualization tools to uncover patterns, trends, and insights.
- **Interpretation**: Translate data findings into actionable insights that inform decision-making.

- **Decision Making**: Make informed choices based on the evidence and evaluate the potential outcomes.
- **Implementation and Monitoring**: Put the decision into action and track its results to measure success.

Challenges and Considerations

- **Data Quality**: Ensuring data accuracy and completeness is crucial for reliable insights.
- **Data Privacy**: Protecting sensitive information is essential when handling personal data.
- **Data Overload**: Managing large volumes of data requires efficient tools and processes.
- **Organizational Culture**: Fostering a data-driven culture requires buy-in from all levels.

Real-World Examples

- **Marketing:** Analyzing customer behavior to optimize ad campaigns and product recommendations.
- **Finance:** Predicting revenue, managing risks, and identifying investment opportunities.
- **Operations:** Improving supply chain efficiency, optimizing inventory levels, and reducing costs.
- **Human Resources:** Hiring the right talent, enhancing employee engagement, and improving retention.

I can provide more detailed examples, discuss data analysis techniques, or delve into the tools and technologies used in DDDM.

Operational Efficiency:

Operational efficiency is the cornerstone of a successful business. It's about maximizing output and minimizing input, or put simply, doing more with less. This involves identifying and eliminating bottlenecks, automating repetitive tasks, and reducing costs while maintaining or improving quality.

Key Components of Operational Efficiency

- **Identifying Bottlenecks:** These are chokepoints in a process that slow down overall performance. They can be identified through process mapping, data analysis, and employee feedback.
- **Process Automation:** Automating repetitive tasks can significantly improve efficiency, reduce errors, and free up employees for more strategic work.
- **Cost Reduction:** Identifying areas of excess spending and implementing strategies to reduce costs without compromising quality is essential.
- **Quality Improvement:** While focusing on efficiency, it's crucial to maintain or enhance product or service quality.

Strategies for Enhancing Operational Efficiency

- **Process Mapping:** Visualizing processes helps identify redundancies, inefficiencies, and potential automation opportunities.
- **Data Analytics:** Leveraging data to understand performance metrics, identify trends, and make data-driven decisions.
- **Lean Methodology:** Implementing lean principles to eliminate waste, improve flow, and create value.
- **Automation:** Employing technologies like Robotic Process Automation (RPA) and artificial intelligence to automate tasks.
- **Employee Empowerment:** Involving employees in process improvement initiatives fosters a culture of innovation.

Examples of Operational Efficiency in Action

- **Manufacturing:** Optimizing production lines, reducing inventory levels, and minimizing downtime.
- **Customer Service:** Implementing self-service options, automating routine inquiries, and reducing average handling time.

- **Finance:** Automating data entry, streamlining approval processes, and reducing errors.
- **Human Resources:** Automating payroll, onboarding, and benefits administration.

The Role of Data-Driven Decision Making

Data plays a pivotal role in operational efficiency. By analyzing performance metrics, businesses can:

- Identify bottlenecks and areas for improvement.
- Measure the impact of automation and process changes.
- Optimize resource allocation.
- Predict future trends and adjust operations accordingly.

Customer Centricity:

Customer centricity is a business philosophy that places the customer at the center of all business decisions. It's about understanding and anticipating customer needs, wants, and desires to deliver exceptional experiences.

Core Components of Customer Centricity

- **Customer Understanding:** Deeply understanding customer behavior, preferences, and motivations.
- **Customer Experience (CX):** Designing and delivering seamless, enjoyable customer journeys.
- **Data-Driven Insights:** Utilizing customer data to inform decisions and personalize experiences.
- **Employee Empowerment:** Equipping employees with the tools and knowledge to deliver exceptional service.

Benefits of Customer Centricity

- **Increased customer loyalty:** Customers are more likely to stay with a brand that genuinely cares about their needs.

- **Improved customer satisfaction:** Meeting or exceeding customer expectations leads to higher satisfaction levels.
- **Higher customer lifetime value:** Loyal customers tend to spend more over time.
- **Stronger brand reputation:** A customer-centric approach builds trust and enhances brand image.

Strategies for Building a Customer-Centric Culture

- **Customer Feedback:** Actively seek and listen to customer feedback through surveys, reviews, and social media.
- **Customer Segmentation:** Divide customers into groups based on shared characteristics to tailor offerings.
- **Personalization:** Deliver customized experiences based on individual preferences and behaviors.
- **Employee Training:** Invest in training employees to understand customer needs and build strong relationships.
- **Customer Journey Mapping:** Visualize the customer experience to identify pain points and opportunities for improvement.

The Role of Technology

Technology plays a crucial role in customer centricity. Tools like:

- **CRM systems:** Manage customer interactions and data.
- **Analytics platforms:** Analyze customer behavior and preferences.
- **Marketing automation:** Personalize communications and campaigns.
- **Customer support tools:** Provide efficient and effective support.

Innovation and Growth:

Innovation and growth are inextricably linked. By discovering new markets, developing groundbreaking products, and optimizing marketing campaigns, businesses can achieve sustainable success.

Key Components of Innovation and Growth

- **Market Research:** Identifying untapped opportunities and understanding customer needs.
- **Product Development:** Creating innovative solutions that address market gaps and deliver value.
- **Marketing Strategy:** Developing effective campaigns to reach the target audience and drive sales.
- **Organizational Culture:** Fostering a culture of creativity, experimentation, and risk-taking.

Strategies for Driving Innovation and Growth

- **Customer-Centric Approach:** Placing the customer at the heart of innovation to develop products that truly resonate.
- **Agile Methodology:** Embracing flexibility and iterative development to accelerate time-to-market.
- **Collaboration:** Fostering partnerships with external innovators to access new ideas and technologies.
- **Experimentation:** Encouraging a culture of experimentation to identify new opportunities.
- **Data-Driven Decision Making:** Using data to inform product development, marketing, and market entry strategies.

The Role of Technology

Technology plays a vital role in innovation and growth. Tools like:

- **AI and machine learning:**Analyzing market trends, predicting customer behavior, and optimizing product design.
- **Big data analytics:** Uncovering hidden insights and identifying new market opportunities.
- **Digital marketing platforms:** Reaching target audiences effectively and measuring campaign performance.
- **Product development software:** Streamlining the product development process and accelerating time-to-market.

Overcoming Challenges

Innovation and growth are not without challenges. Overcoming obstacles like:

- **Fear of failure:** Creating a safe space for experimentation and learning from mistakes.
- **Resource constraints:** Prioritizing initiatives and optimizing resource allocation.
- **Competitive pressures:** Differentiating offerings and building a strong brand identity.

Risk Management:

- Risk management is the systematic process of identifying, assessing, and controlling potential threats to an organization's objectives.
- It's about making informed decisions to minimize the impact of negative events.

Key Components of Risk Management

- **Risk Identification:** Recognizing potential threats that could impact the organization.
- **Risk Assessment:** Evaluating the likelihood and potential impact of identified risks.
- **Risk Mitigation:** Developing strategies to reduce the impact or probability of risks occurring.
- **Risk Monitoring and Control:** Continuously tracking risks and adjusting mitigation plans as needed.

Types of Risks

- **Operational risks:** Internal processes, systems, or people failures.

- **Financial risks:** Economic conditions, market fluctuations, credit risks.
- **Strategic risks:** Changes in market conditions, competition, or technology.
- **Reputational risks:** Negative publicity, customer dissatisfaction, or legal issues.

Risk Management Strategies

- **Risk Avoidance:** Eliminating the risk altogether.
- **Risk Reduction:** Implementing measures to reduce the likelihood or impact of a risk.
- **Risk Transfer:** Shifting the risk to a third party (e.g., insurance).
- **Risk Acceptance:** Acknowledging the risk and deciding to bear the potential consequences.

The Role of Technology

Technology can significantly enhance risk management capabilities:

- **Risk assessment tools:** Quantifying and prioritizing risks.
- **Data analytics:** Identifying patterns and trends in risk data.
- **Cybersecurity solutions:** Protecting against cyber threats.
- **Business continuity planning software:** Developing and testing disaster recovery plans.

Benefits of Big Data-Driven Transformation

Increased Profitability

- **Revenue Growth:** Identifying new market segments, optimizing pricing strategies, and increasing sales.
- **Cost Reduction:** Streamlining operations, reducing waste, and optimizing resource allocation.
- **Profit Margin Improvement:** Enhancing product margins and pricing strategies.

Improved Customer Satisfaction

- **Personalized Experiences:** Tailoring products and services to individual customer preferences.
- **Enhanced Customer Service:** Providing timely and relevant support.
- **Customer Loyalty:** Building strong customer relationships through value-added interactions.

Enhanced Operational Efficiency

- **Supply Chain Optimization:** Improving inventory management and logistics.
- **Process Improvement:** Identifying bottlenecks and streamlining workflows.
- **Resource Optimization:** Allocating resources effectively based on data-driven insights.

Competitive Advantage

- **Market Leadership:** Gaining a first-mover advantage through data-driven innovation.
- **Differentiation:** Offering unique products and services based on customer insights.
- **Risk Mitigation:** Identifying and addressing potential threats before they impact the business.

Accelerated Innovation

- **New Product Development:** Identifying market gaps and developing innovative solutions.
- **Product Optimization:** Enhancing existing products based on customer feedback and usage data.
- **Faster Time-to-Market:** Bringing products to market more quickly through data-driven insights.

By focusing on these areas, organizations can unlock the full potential of big data and drive significant business transformation. By embracing big data analytics, organizations can unlock their full potential and thrive in the digital age.

Customer Insights:

Understanding customer behavior through Big Data is the cornerstone of creating exceptional customer experiences. By analyzing vast amounts of data, businesses can gain profound insights into customer preferences, needs, and buying patterns. This knowledge empowers organizations to:

- **Tailor products and services:** Create offerings that precisely align with customer desires and expectations.
- **Optimize marketing campaigns:** Deliver targeted messages to the right audience at the right time.
- **Enhance customer service:** Provide timely and relevant support based on customer interactions.
- **Identify new market opportunities:** Discover untapped segments and develop innovative products.

Key data points that contribute to a comprehensive customer view include:

- **Demographic information:** Age, gender, location, income.
- **Purchase history:** Product preferences, buying patterns, and spending habits.
- **Online behavior:** Website visits, social media interactions, and search history.
- **Customer feedback:** Reviews, surveys, and customer support interactions.

By harnessing the power of big data, businesses can transform customer insights into a competitive advantage.

Innovation:

Big data serves as the catalyst for innovation, propelling businesses into new frontiers. By uncovering hidden patterns and trends within vast datasets, organizations can:

- **Identify new market opportunities:** Discover untapped segments and customer needs.
- **Develop innovative products and services:** Create solutions that address unmet customer demands.
- **Optimize product development:** Refine product features based on user feedback and usage data.
- **Experiment and iterate rapidly:** Test new ideas and business models at scale.
- **Create new business models:** Leverage data to develop entirely new revenue streams.

Examples of innovation driven by big data:

- **Netflix:** Using viewing data to create original content and personalized recommendations.
- **Amazon:** Leveraging purchase history to suggest products and introduce new services like Amazon Web Services.
- **Uber:** Utilizing location data and user preferences to revolutionize transportation.

By embracing a culture of experimentation and data-driven innovation, organizations can unlock the full potential of big data and achieve sustainable growth.

Social Impact:

Big data has the potential to be a powerful tool for addressing some of the world's most pressing challenges. By harnessing the power of data, governments, non-profit organizations, and businesses can develop innovative solutions to improve lives and protect our planet.

Key areas of social impact:

- **Education:** Personalizing learning experiences, optimizing resource allocation, and improving student outcomes.
- **Climate Change:** Analyzing climate patterns, predicting natural disasters, and developing sustainable solutions.
- **Poverty Reduction:** Identifying vulnerable populations, optimizing social programs, and promoting economic growth.
- **Disaster Response:** Improving emergency response and recovery efforts through real-time data analysis.

By leveraging big data, we can create a more equitable, sustainable, and resilient world.

Challenges of Big Data

- **Data Storage:** Managing and storing vast amounts of data requires efficient and scalable solutions.
- **Data Processing:** Processing Big Data demands powerful computing resources and specialized algorithms.
- **Data Analysis:** Extracting valuable insights from complex data sets requires advanced analytics techniques.
- **Data Security and Privacy:** Protecting sensitive data is paramount due to increasing cyber threats.

By understanding the nature and implications of Big Data, organizations can harness its potential to gain a competitive advantage and drive positive change.

Importance of Big Data Analytics

Big Data Analytics is the process of examining large volumes of data to uncover hidden patterns, correlations, and other useful information. It's the engine that drives data-driven decision making.

Why is Big Data Analytics Crucial?

- **Improved Decision Making:** By analyzing vast datasets, organizations can identify trends, predict outcomes, and make informed decisions.

- **Enhanced Customer Experience:** Understanding customer behavior through data helps businesses tailor products, services, and marketing campaigns.
- **Operational Efficiency:** Big Data Analytics can optimize processes, reduce costs, and improve overall efficiency.
- **New Product Development:** Identifying market gaps and customer preferences can lead to innovative product offerings.
- **Risk Management:** By analyzing historical data, organizations can identify potential risks and develop mitigation strategies.
- **Competitive Advantage:** Businesses that leverage Big Data Analytics effectively gain a significant edge over competitors.

Real-World Applications

- **Healthcare:** Identifying disease outbreaks, optimizing treatment plans, and developing new drugs.
- **Finance:** Detecting fraud, managing risk, and predicting market trends.
- **Retail:** Personalizing recommendations, optimizing inventory, and improving customer loyalty.
- **Marketing:** Targeting the right audience, measuring campaign effectiveness, and optimizing marketing spend.
- **Government:** Improving public services, managing infrastructure, and preventing crime.

In essence, Big Data Analytics is a powerful tool that can transform businesses and society. By harnessing the potential of data, organizations can unlock new opportunities, improve performance, and create value.

Challenges in Big Data Analytics

While Big Data offers immense potential, it also presents significant challenges:

Data Volume, Variety, and Velocity

- **Handling Massive Datasets:** Storing and processing petabytes or exabytes of data requires specialized infrastructure and efficient algorithms.
- **Diverse Data Formats:** Integrating data from various sources (structured, unstructured, and semi-structured) is complex and time-consuming.
- **Real-time Processing:** Extracting insights from rapidly incoming data streams is technically demanding and requires low-latency systems.

Data Quality and Integrity

- **Inconsistent Data:** Data from different sources often has varying formats, quality, and accuracy, leading to inconsistencies.
- **Data Cleaning and Preparation:** Cleaning and preparing data for analysis is time-consuming and resource-intensive.
- **Missing Data:** Incomplete datasets can impact the accuracy of analysis and insights.

Data Security and Privacy

- **Sensitive Information:** Protecting sensitive data from unauthorized access, breaches, and misuse is crucial.
- **Compliance:** Adhering to data privacy regulations (e.g., GDPR, CCPA) is complex and requires ongoing efforts.
- **Data Governance:** Establishing clear data ownership, access controls, and usage policies is essential.

Talent Shortage

- **Skilled Professionals:** Finding data scientists, analysts, and engineers with the necessary expertise is challenging.
- **Training and Development:** Investing in employee training and development is crucial to build a skilled workforce.

Infrastructure and Cost

- **Expensive Technology:** Implementing Big Data solutions can be costly due to hardware, software, and infrastructure requirements.
- **Scalability:** Ensuring that the infrastructure can handle increasing data volumes and processing demands is essential.

Lack of Standardization

- **Diverse Tools and Technologies:** The Big Data ecosystem lacks standardization, making it difficult to compare and integrate different solutions.
- **Interoperability:** Integrating various Big Data tools and platforms can be challenging due to compatibility issues.

Addressing these challenges requires a combination of technological advancements, skilled professionals, and robust data management practices.

CHAPTER THREE

UNDERSTANDING BIG DATA

The 5 V's of Big Data

The 5 V's of Big Data are essential characteristics that define the nature and complexity of large datasets.

Volume

- **Definition:** The sheer amount of data generated.
- **Implications:** Requires efficient storage and processing capabilities.
    - Example: Petabytes or exabytes of data generated by social media, IoT devices, and online transactions.

Velocity

- **Definition:** The speed at which data is generated and processed.
- **Implications:** Demands real-time or near-real-time analytics.
    - Example: Financial market data, social media feeds, and sensor data.

Variety

- **Definition:** The different types of data, both structured and unstructured.
- **Implications:** Requires flexible data management and processing tools.
    - Example: Text, images, audio, video, and sensor data.

Veracity

- **Definition:** The quality, accuracy, and reliability of the data.
- **Implications:** Impacts the trustworthiness of insights derived from the data.
    - Example: Social media sentiment analysis, where data can be biased or subjective.

Value

- **Definition:** The potential of the data to generate business value or insights.
- **Implications:** Drives the investment in Big Data initiatives.
    - Example: Improved customer experience, increased revenue, and operational efficiency.

Understanding these characteristics is crucial for organizations to effectively manage and leverage Big Data to gain a competitive advantage.

Big Data Ecosystem

A Big Data Ecosystem is a complex network of technologies, tools, and processes that work together to capture, store, process, analyze, and derive value from large volumes of data. It's a comprehensive environment that enables organizations to handle the challenges and opportunities presented by Big Data.

Key Components of a Big Data Ecosystem

Data Sources:

Data is the lifeblood of modern businesses and organizations. Its origins are diverse and ever-expanding. Let's explore some of the primary data sources:

Traditional Data Sources

- **Databases:** Structured repositories of information, typically relational (like SQL databases) or NoSQL (for unstructured data).
  - Examples: Customer databases, financial records, inventory management systems.
- **Spreadsheets:** Simple yet powerful tools for storing and analyzing data.
  - Examples: Sales figures, project timelines, financial forecasts.

Digital Data Sources

- **Social Media:** A rich source of unstructured data about people, trends, and sentiments.
  - Examples: Facebook, Twitter, Instagram, LinkedIn.
- **Websites:** Web analytics provide insights into user behavior, traffic patterns, and conversions.
  - Examples: Google Analytics, website logs.
- **E-commerce Platforms:** Data on customer purchases, preferences, and browsing behavior.
  - Examples: Amazon, eBay, online retailers.

Emerging Data Sources

- **IoT Devices:** Connected devices generating vast amounts of real-time data.
    - Examples: Smart homes, wearables, industrial sensors.
- **Sensors:** Devices that capture data from the physical world.
    - Examples: Temperature sensors, motion detectors, air quality monitors.
- **Mobile Devices:** Smartphones and tablets generate location, app usage, and user behavior data.
- **GPS Data:** Location-based information from GPS-enabled devices.
- **Satellite Imagery:** Data from satellites for various applications like agriculture, disaster management, and urban planning.

Other Data Sources

- **Government and Public Data:** Census data, economic indicators, weather data.
- **Transactional Data:** Data generated from business transactions (e.g., point-of-sale data).
- **Customer Surveys and Feedback:** Valuable insights into customer opinions and preferences.

Key Considerations for Data Sources

- **Data Quality:** Ensuring data accuracy, completeness, and consistency.
- **Data Privacy:** Adhering to data protection regulations (e.g., GDPR, CCPA).

- **Data Security:** Protecting data from unauthorized access and breaches.
- **Data Integration:** Combining data from various sources for comprehensive analysis.
- **Data Governance:** Establishing data standards and policies for effective management.

By understanding the diverse range of data sources available, organizations can harness the power of data to drive informed decision-making, improve operations, and gain a competitive edge.

Data Ingestion:

Data ingestion is indeed the crucial first step in the data lifecycle. It involves capturing raw data from diverse sources, transforming it into a usable format, and loading it into a designated storage system for further processing and analysis.

Key Stages of Data Ingestion

Data Extraction: This is the process of retrieving data from various sources.

- **Methods:** APIs, database queries, file transfers, web scraping, and more.

Data Transformation: Raw data is often unstructured or inconsistent. This stage involves cleaning, standardizing, and converting data into a suitable format for analysis.

- **Activities:** Data cleaning, normalization, enrichment, and aggregation.

Data Loading: The transformed data is moved into a target system like a data warehouse, data lake, or database for storage and processing.

- **Methods:** Batch loading, incremental loading, and real-time loading.

Challenges in Data Ingestion

- **Data Quality:** Ensuring data accuracy, completeness, and consistency.
- **Data Volume:** Handling large volumes of data efficiently.
- **Data Velocity:** Processing data in real-time or near-real-time.
- **Data Variety:** Dealing with structured, unstructured, and semi-structured data.
- **Data Integration:** Combining data from multiple sources.

Tools and Technologies

To streamline the data ingestion process, organizations often leverage:

- **ETL (Extract, Transform, Load):** Traditional approach for batch data processing.
- **ELT (Extract, Load, Transform):** Suitable for large datasets and cloud-based environments.
- **Data Integration Platforms:** Tools for connecting and managing data from various sources.
- **Data Pipelines:** Automated workflows for data ingestion and transformation.
- **Big Data Technologies:** Handling massive volumes of data (Hadoop, Spark).

By effectively managing the data ingestion process, organizations can lay a strong foundation for data-driven decision-making and gain valuable insights from their data assets.

Data Storage:

Data storage is the cornerstone of any data-driven initiative. It encompasses the systems and technologies designed to hold vast amounts of data, ensuring its accessibility, reliability, and durability.

Key Data Storage Systems

- **Hadoop Distributed File System (HDFS):**

  - Designed for storing massive amounts of unstructured data.
  - Highly fault-tolerant, scalable, and cost-effective.
  - Ideal for batch processing and analytics workloads.

- **NoSQL Databases:**
  - Non-relational databases that handle diverse data structures and large volumes of data.
  - Offer flexibility, scalability, and high performance.
  - Examples: MongoDB, Cassandra, Redis.

- **Cloud Storage:**
  - Scalable, cost-effective, and accessible data storage solutions provided by cloud providers.
  - Offer various storage options like object storage, block storage, and file storage.
  - Examples: Amazon S3, Google Cloud Storage, Azure Blob Storage.

- **Data Warehouses:**
  - Centralized repositories for structured data, optimized for complex queries and reporting.
  - Support business intelligence and analytics applications.

- **Data Lakes:**
  - Scalable storage repositories for both structured and unstructured data.
  - Serve as a landing zone for raw data before processing and analysis.

Key Considerations for Data Storage

- **Data Volume:** The amount of data to be stored.
- **Data Variety:** The different types of data (structured, unstructured, semi-structured).
- **Data Velocity:** The speed at which data is generated and processed.
- **Data Veracity:** The quality and reliability of the data.
- **Data Value:** The potential insights and benefits derived from the data.
- **Cost:** The cost of storing and managing data.
- **Performance:** The speed at which data can be accessed and processed.
- **Scalability:** The ability to handle increasing data volumes.
- **Security:** Protecting data from unauthorized access and breaches.

By carefully selecting the appropriate data storage system based on these factors, organizations can effectively manage their data assets and unlock valuable insights.

Data Processing: Tools and frameworks for processing large datasets, including Hadoop MapReduce, Apache Spark, and cloud-based computing platforms.

Data Analysis:

Data analysis is the process of examining raw data to draw conclusions about the information it contains. It involves applying various techniques and algorithms to extract meaningful insights, patterns, and trends.

Core Components of Data Analysis

- **Data Mining:** The process of discovering patterns in large data sets involving methods at the intersection of machine learning, statistics, and database systems.
  - Techniques: Association rule learning, clustering, classification, regression.

- **Machine Learning:** A subset of artificial intelligence that allows systems to learn and improve from experience without being explicitly programmed.
    - Algorithms: Decision trees, random forests, support vector machines, neural networks.
- **Statistical Analysis:** The application of statistical methods to collect, organize, analyze, interpret, and present data.
    - Techniques: Descriptive statistics, inferential statistics, hypothesis testing.

Types of Data Analysis

- **Descriptive Analytics:** Summarizes past data to understand what has happened.
- **Diagnostic Analytics:** Investigates the root causes of past events.
- **Predictive Analytics:** Uses historical data to predict future outcomes.
- **Prescriptive Analytics:** Recommends actions based on predictive models.

Challenges in Data Analysis

- **Data Quality:** Ensuring data accuracy, completeness, and consistency.
- **Data Volume:** Handling large datasets efficiently.
- **Data Variety:** Dealing with structured, unstructured, and semi-structured data.
- **Data Velocity:** Processing data in real-time or near-real-time.

Tools and Technologies

- **Statistical Software:** SPSS, SAS, R, Python (with libraries like NumPy, pandas, SciPy, Statsmodels).
- **Machine Learning Libraries:** Scikit-learn, TensorFlow, PyTorch.
- **Data Visualization Tools:** Tableau, Power BI, matplotlib, seaborn.
- **Big Data Platforms:** Hadoop, Spark.

By effectively applying data analysis techniques, organizations can gain a competitive advantage, optimize operations, and make data-driven decisions.

Data Visualization:

Data visualization is the art and science of communicating data through visual representations. It transforms complex information into easily understandable formats, allowing audiences to grasp insights quickly and effectively.

Key Components of Data Visualization

- **Charts and Graphs:** Visual representations of data relationships, including:
  - Bar charts: Comparing categories.
  - Line charts: Showing trends over time.
  - Scatter plots: Identifying correlations between variables.
  - Pie charts: Representing proportions of a whole.
  - Histograms: Displaying frequency distributions.
- **Dashboards:** Interactive displays of key performance indicators (KPIs) and other relevant data.
- **Infographics:** Visualizations that combine text, images, and charts to tell a story.
- **Maps:** Geographical representations of data.

Benefits of Data Visualization

- **Improved understanding:** Visuals make complex data easier to comprehend.
- **Faster insights:** Visuals help identify patterns and trends quickly.
- **Effective communication:** Visuals can tell compelling stories with data.
- **Data exploration:** Visualizations facilitate interactive exploration of data.
- **Decision making:** Visuals support informed decision-making.

Challenges in Data Visualization

- **Data complexity:** Handling large and diverse datasets.
- **Visual clutter:** Avoiding overwhelming viewers with too much information.
- **Data storytelling:** Creating engaging and informative narratives.
- **Accessibility:** Ensuring visualizations are understandable to all audiences.

Tools and Technologies

- **Business Intelligence (BI) Tools:** Tableau, Power BI, Qlik.
- **Data Visualization Libraries:** Python (Matplotlib, Seaborn, Plotly), R (ggplot2), JavaScript (D3.js).
- **Specialized Visualization Tools:** Geographic Information Systems (GIS), statistical software.

By effectively utilizing data visualization, organizations can communicate insights clearly, make informed decisions, and drive business success.

Data Governance:

Data governance is the overarching framework for managing and utilizing an organization's data. It ensures data quality, security, compliance, and overall value. It's about establishing clear policies, roles, and responsibilities for data across its lifecycle.

Key Components of Data Governance

- **Data Quality:** Ensuring data is accurate, complete, consistent, relevant, timely, and accessible.
- **Data Security:** Protecting data from unauthorized access, use, disclosure, disruption, modification, or destruction.
- **Data Privacy:** Safeguarding individuals' personal information and complying with privacy regulations (GDPR, CCPA, etc.).
- **Data Compliance:** Adhering to industry-specific regulations and standards (HIPAA, SOX, PCI DSS).
- **Data Retention and Deletion:** Defining data lifecycle management policies, including retention periods and disposal methods.
- **Data Ownership and Stewardship:** Assigning responsibilities for data management and protection.
- **Metadata Management:** Ensuring accurate and up-to-date information about data.

Benefits of Effective Data Governance

- **Improved data quality:** Leading to better decision-making and operational efficiency.
- **Enhanced data security:** Protecting sensitive information and mitigating risks.
- **Stronger compliance posture:** Reducing the risk of fines and penalties.
- **Increased trust:** Building confidence in data and its use.
- **Optimized data utilization:** Maximizing the value of data assets.

Challenges in Data Governance

- **Data silos:** Overcoming data isolation across departments.
- **Data quality issues:** Addressing inconsistencies and inaccuracies.

- **Regulatory complexity:** Keeping up with evolving compliance requirements.
- **Organizational culture:** Fostering a data-centric mindset.

Tools and Technologies

- **Data Governance Platforms:** Centralized platforms for managing data policies, metadata, and access controls.
- **Data Quality Tools:** Software for assessing and improving data quality.
- **Data Security Tools:** Solutions for protecting data from threats.
- **Compliance Management Tools:** Software for tracking and managing compliance obligations.

Key Technologies in the Big Data Ecosystem

- **Hadoop Ecosystem:** A collection of open-source software frameworks for storing, processing, and analyzing large datasets.
- **NoSQL Databases:** Designed to handle unstructured and semi-structured data, offering scalability and flexibility.
- **Cloud Computing Platforms:** Provide infrastructure, platforms, and software as services for Big Data processing and analysis.
- **Data Warehouses and Data Lakes:** Centralized repositories for storing and managing data.
- **Business Intelligence (BI) Tools:** For interactive exploration and analysis of data.

Challenges and Opportunities

- **Data Quality:** Ensuring data accuracy and consistency is crucial for reliable insights.
- **Data Security:** Protecting sensitive data from breaches is paramount.
- **Talent Acquisition:** Finding skilled professionals to manage and analyze Big Data is challenging.

- **Cost Management:** Implementing and maintaining a Big Data infrastructure can be expensive.

Despite these challenges, the potential benefits of Big Data are immense. Organizations can gain valuable insights, improve decision-making, enhance customer experiences, and drive innovation through effective utilization of the Big Data ecosystem.

Data Lakes vs. Data Warehouses

Data lakes and data warehouses are both essential components of a modern data management strategy, but they serve distinct purposes.

Data Lake

- **Definition:** A centralized repository that stores raw data in its native format, without any predefined schema. It's like a vast digital lake that collects data from various sources.
- **Characteristics:**
    - Stores all types of data (structured, unstructured, and semi-structured).
    - Schema-on-read approach, where data is structured when queried.
    - High volume, velocity, and variety of data.
    - Ideal for exploratory data analysis, machine learning, and data science projects.
    - Often used for long-term data retention and archiving.

Data Warehouse

- **Definition:** A centralized repository for structured data that has been cleaned, transformed, and integrated for analytical purposes. It's like a well-organized warehouse with specific products (data) ready for consumption.
- **Characteristics:**

- Stores structured data optimized for querying and reporting.
- Schema-on-write approach, where data is structured during ingestion.
- Focuses on historical data for reporting and analysis.
- Supports business intelligence and reporting tools.
- Often used for operational reporting and decision-making.

Data Lake: When you need to store large volumes of raw data, explore new insights, or support machine learning projects.

- **Data Warehouse:** When you need to support business intelligence, reporting, and decision-making based on structured data.

Often, organizations use a combination of both data lakes and data warehouses. Data can be extracted from the data lake, processed, and loaded into a data warehouse for further analysis and reporting. This hybrid approach provides flexibility and efficiency.

CHAPTER FOUR

BIG DATA TOOLS AND TECHNOLOGIES

The Hadoop Ecosystem

Hadoop is a robust framework designed to process vast amounts of data across clusters of computers using simple programming models. It's composed of several interconnected components, collectively known as the Hadoop Ecosystem.

Core Components

HDFS (Hadoop Distributed File System)

- The foundation of Hadoop.
- Stores data in a distributed manner across multiple nodes.
- Provides high fault tolerance and scalability.
- Optimized for large file handling and appends.

MapReduce

- A programming model for processing large datasets.
- Breaks down tasks into Map and Reduce phases.

- Handles data distribution and processing efficiently.

YARN (Yet Another Resource Negotiator)

- The resource manager for Hadoop.
- Manages cluster resources and schedules applications.
- Separates resource management from application management.

Data Processing Tools

Hive

- Provides SQL-like interface to query data stored in HDFS.
- Converts SQL queries into MapReduce jobs.
- Enables data warehousing and analysis on Hadoop.

Pig

- High-level scripting language for data analysis.
- Offers a more expressive and flexible approach than MapReduce.
- Simplifies data transformation and aggregation.

Spark

- In-memory data processing engine.
- Significantly faster than MapReduce for iterative algorithms and real-time processing.
- Supports SQL, machine learning, and graph processing.

HBase

- NoSQL database built on top of HDFS.
- Offers fast random read and write access.
- Ideal for large-scale, real-time applications.

Other Important Components

- **Zookeeper:** Used for coordination and configuration management in Hadoop clusters.
- **Oozie:** Workflow scheduler for managing Hadoop jobs.
- **Sqoop:** Transfers data between Hadoop and relational databases.
- **Mahout:** Machine learning library for Hadoop.

How the Hadoop Ecosystem Works Together

The components you've mentioned work in concert to form a robust big data processing platform.

Let's break down their roles:

Storage: HDFS and HBase

- **HDFS (Hadoop Distributed File System):** This is the foundation for storing massive amounts of data across multiple nodes. It's optimized for large files and batch processing.
- **HBase:** For scenarios demanding fast random access to structured data, HBase, a NoSQL database built on HDFS, provides a high-performance solution. It's suitable for real-time applications.

Processing: MapReduce and Spark

- **MapReduce:** A programming model for processing large datasets across clusters of computers. It's well-suited for batch processing.
- **Spark:** A faster and more general engine for large-scale data processing. It supports both batch and stream processing, making it versatile.

Resource Management: YARN

- **YARN (Yet Another Resource Negotiator):** Acts as the resource manager for Hadoop clusters. It allocates resources like CPU, memory, and disk to applications running on the cluster. This ensures efficient utilization of resources.

Data Querying: Hive and Pig

- **Hive:** Provides a SQL-like interface to query data stored in HDFS. It translates SQL statements into MapReduce jobs, making it accessible to SQL-savvy users.
- **Pig:** Offers a higher-level scripting language for data analysis. It's more flexible than Hive for complex data transformations.

The Workflow

1. **Data Ingestion:** Data is collected from various sources and stored in HDFS.
2. **Data Processing:** MapReduce or Spark processes the data based on the specific task. YARN allocates resources for these jobs.
3. **Data Querying:** Hive or Pig is used to query the processed data, often stored in HDFS or HBase.
4. **Data Analysis:** The results of queries can be further analyzed using statistical tools or machine learning algorithms.
5. **Data Visualization:** Tools like Tableau or Power BI can be used to visualize the insights derived from the data.

Key Points

- **Complementary Roles:** Each component plays a specific role, but they work together seamlessly.
- **Scalability:** The distributed nature of these components allows for handling massive datasets and complex workloads.
- **Fault Tolerance:** The system is designed to handle failures and continue processing.

- **Cost-Efficiency:** Leveraging commodity hardware for storage and processing.

NoSQL Databases: MongoDB, Cassandra, and Couchbase

- NoSQL databases emerged as a response to the limitations of traditional relational databases in handling massive, unstructured, and rapidly growing datasets.
- They offer flexibility, scalability, and performance advantages for various applications. Let's explore three of the most popular NoSQL databases: MongoDB, Cassandra, and Couchbase.

MongoDB:

- **Flexibility**: The schema-less nature allows for rapid application development and easy adaptation to changing data requirements.
- **Scalability**: MongoDB can handle massive datasets and high-throughput workloads efficiently.
- **Performance**: Its indexing capabilities and in-memory storage options contribute to fast query performance.
- **High Availability**: MongoDB offers replication and sharding for data redundancy and fault tolerance.

Common Use Cases

- **Content Management Systems (CMS)**: Storing complex content structures like articles, images, and metadata.
- **Real-time Analytics**: Processing and analyzing large volumes of data for insights.
- **Mobile and IoT Applications**: Handling diverse data structures and high-velocity data streams.
- **Gaming**: Managing user profiles, game data, and real-time interactions.

- **E-commerce**: Storing product catalogs, user preferences, and order information.

Additional Features

- **Aggregation Pipeline**: For complex data processing and analysis.
- **Full-Text Search**: For efficient searching within textual data.
- **Geospatial Indexing**: For location-based services and applications.

Cassandra

- Wide-column store.
- Designed for high availability and scalability.
- Handles massive amounts of data with low latency.
- Offers eventual consistency, making it suitable for high-write workloads.
- Ideal for applications requiring high performance and fault tolerance.

Couchbase

- Document-oriented database with key-value store capabilities.
- Combines flexibility with high performance.
- Offers a rich feature set including indexing, full-text search, and caching.
- Supports both JSON and binary data formats.
- Ideal for applications demanding fast read and write operations and complex data modeling.

Choosing the Right NoSQL Database

The best NoSQL database depends on specific application requirements. Consider the following factors:

- **Data structure:** How complex is your data?

- **Data volume and growth:** How much data do you expect to handle?
- **Query patterns:** What types of queries will you perform?
- **Consistency requirements:** How important is strong consistency?
- **Performance needs:** What level of performance is required?
- By carefully evaluating these factors, you can select the NoSQL database that best aligns with your application's needs.

CHAPTER FIVE

CLOUD-BASED BIG DATA SOLUTIONS

The cloud has revolutionized how organizations handle Big Data.Major cloud providers like AWS, Azure, and GCP offer a comprehensive suite of services to manage, process, and analyze large datasets. Understanding Storage Options: Object Storage, Data Lakes, and Data Warehouses

Object Storage

Key Characteristics:

- Stores data as objects, each with metadata and a unique identifier.
- Highly scalable, durable, and cost-effective for large amounts of unstructured data.
- Ideal for storing backups, archives, images, videos, and log files.

- **Examples:** Amazon S3, Azure Blob Storage, Google Cloud Storage.

Data Lakes

- **Key Characteristics:**

- A centralized repository for storing raw data in its native format.
- Combines aspects of data warehouses and object stores.
- Supports both structured and unstructured data.
- Often built on top of object storage for scalability and cost-efficiency.
- Ideal for data exploration, machine learning, and big data analytics.

- **Examples:** Amazon S3, Azure Data Lake Storage, Google Cloud Storage.

Data Warehouses

- **Key Characteristics:**
    - Optimized for analytical workloads and reporting.
    - Stores structured data in a relational format.
    - Supports complex queries and aggregations.
    - Often used for business intelligence and reporting.

- **Examples:** Amazon Redshift, Google BigQuery, Snowflake.

When to Use Which

- **Object Storage:** Best for storing large amounts of unstructured data that doesn't require frequent analysis.
- **Data Lake:** Ideal for storing raw data for future exploration and analysis.
- **Data Warehouse:** Suitable for storing structured data for reporting and business intelligence.
- Often, a combination of these storage options is used in a data architecture. For example, data can be ingested into a data lake for initial storage, then processed and transformed into a data warehouse for analytical purposes.

Overview of Cloud-Based Big Data Solutions

These platforms provide a range of services, including:

- **Data Processing:** Distributed computing frameworks (Hadoop, Spark), serverless computing.
- **Data Analytics:** SQL and NoSQL databases, machine learning, data warehousing.
- **Data Governance:** Security, compliance, and data management tools.
-

Key Services and Use Cases

Storage

- **Object Storage:**Store vast amounts of unstructured data (S3, Blob Storage, Cloud Storage) for images, videos, logs, and more.
- **Data Lakes:** Create centralized repositories for raw data (Amazon S3, Azure Data Lake Storage, Google Cloud Storage) to enable data exploration and discovery.
- **Data Warehouses:** Build enterprise data warehouses for reporting and analytics (Amazon Redshift, Azure Synapse Analytics, BigQuery).
- *Data Processing*
- **Distributed Computing:** Process large datasets using Hadoop or Spark clusters (EMR, HDInsight, Dataproc).
- **Serverless Computing:**Execute code without managing infrastructure (AWS Lambda, Azure Functions, Google Cloud Functions).
- *Data Analytics*
- **SQL and NoSQL Databases:** Store and query structured and unstructured data (Amazon RDS, Azure SQL Database, Cloud SQL; DynamoDB, Cassandra, MongoDB).
- **Machine Learning:**Build, train, and deploy machine learning models (SageMaker, Azure Machine Learning, Cloud AI).
- **Data Warehousing:** Analyze large datasets for business intelligence and reporting (Redshift, Synapse Analytics,

BigQuery).

- *Choosing the Right Cloud Platform*

Selecting the best cloud platform depends on various factors:

- **Workload requirements:** Consider the nature and volume of your data, processing needs, and performance expectations.
- **Existing infrastructure:** Evaluate compatibility with your on-premises systems and applications.
- **Cost:** Compare pricing models and total cost of ownership.
- **Vendor lock-in:** Assess the ease of migrating data and applications to other platforms.
- **Security and compliance:** Evaluate the security features and compliance certifications offered by each provider.
- By carefully considering these factors, you can choose the cloud platform that best suits your organization's Big Data needs.

CHAPTER SIX

DATA INTEGRATION AND ETL TOOLS

Understanding ETL

ETL (Extract, Transform, Load) is a critical process in data integration.

It involves:

- **Extracting** data from various sources like databases, files, APIs, and applications.
- **Transforming** data by cleaning, standardizing, and converting it into a suitable format for the target system.
- **Loading** the transformed data into a data warehouse, data mart, or other target system.

The Role of ETL Tools

ETL tools streamline the data integration process by providing a graphical interface, pre-built connectors, and automation capabilities. They help to:

- **Improve data quality:**By cleaning and standardizing data before loading.
- **Enhance data consistency:**By ensuring data uniformity across different systems.
- **Accelerate data integration:** By automating routine tasks and reducing manual effort.

- **Support complex transformations:** By offering advanced data manipulation functions.

Popular ETL Tools

The ETL landscape is vast, with tools catering to different needs and budgets. Here are some prominent options:

Open-Source Tools

- **Talend Open Studio:** Offers a comprehensive suite of data integration features.
- **Pentaho Data Integration:** Provides a user-friendly interface and strong community support.
- **Apache Airflow:**A platform for programming and managing workflows.

Commercial Tools

- **Informatica Power Center:** Industry-leading ETL tool with extensive features.
- **IBM Info Sphere Data Stage:** Known for its scalability and performance.
- **Oracle Data Integrator:** Tightly integrated with Oracle database environment.
- **Microsoft SQL Server Integration Services (SSIS):** Part of the SQL Server ecosystem.

Cloud-Based Tools

- **AWS Glue:**Serverless ETL service for building data pipelines.
- **Azure Data Factory:** Cloud-based ETL service for creating and managing data integration pipelines.
- **Google Cloud Dataflow:**Fully managed service for data ingestion, processing, and analysis.

Key Considerations for Choosing an ETL Tool

Data Sources and Targets:

Data compatibility is a critical aspect of any data-driven initiative. It involves ensuring that data can be seamlessly transferred, transformed, and utilized between different systems and applications.

Key Considerations for Compatibility:

- Data Formats: Compatibility at the most basic level involves matching data formats. Common formats include CSV, JSON, XML, Parquet, and Avro. Ensuring source and target systems can handle these formats is essential.
- Data Structures: Understanding the underlying data structures is crucial. Relational databases, NoSQL databases, and data lakes have different structures. Mapping data between these structures requires careful planning.
- Data Types: Data types should align between systems. For example, a numeric data type in one system should not be converted to a string in another without proper handling.
- Data Quality: Inconsistent data quality can hinder compatibility. Data cleaning and standardization are essential before integration.
- Data Volume and Velocity: The volume and speed of data transfer must be considered. High-volume or real-time data streams require specialized tools and infrastructure.
- Metadata: Consistent metadata management is crucial for understanding data meaning and context across systems.

Common Compatibility Challenges:

- Data Schema Mismatches: Different systems may have varying data structures and schemas.
- Data Quality Issues: Inconsistent or inaccurate data can lead to errors and inconsistencies.
- Data Loss or Corruption: Data transformation and migration processes can introduce errors.

- Performance Bottlenecks: Inefficient data transfer can impact system performance.

Strategies for Ensuring Compatibility:

- Data Mapping: Creating a detailed mapping between source and target data elements.
- Data Transformation: Applying rules and logic to convert data from one format to another.
- Data Cleansing: Identifying and correcting data errors and inconsistencies.
- Data Standardization: Enforcing consistent data formats and definitions.
- Data Integration Tools: Utilizing ETL or ELT tools to automate data transfer and transformation.
- Testing and Validation: Thoroughly testing the data integration process to identify and resolve issues.

Examples of Data Sources and Targets:

- CRM systems to data warehouses: Extracting customer data for analysis and reporting.
- IoT devices to cloud storage: Collecting sensor data for storage and processing.
- Social media platforms to data lakes: Gathering public data for sentiment analysis.
- Legacy systems to modern data platforms: Migrating data to improve accessibility and performance.

By carefully considering these factors and implementing appropriate strategies, organizations can effectively manage data compatibility and unlock the full potential of their data assets.

Data Volume and Complexity:

Data volume and complexity have exploded in recent years, presenting significant challenges for organizations. Handling massive datasets while maintaining high performance is crucial for extracting valuable insights.

Key Considerations:

Data Volume

- Scalability: The ability to handle increasing data volumes without compromising performance.
    - Hrizontal scaling (adding more nodes) is often preferred for big data.
    - Vertical scaling (increasing resurces of existing nodes) might be suitable for smaller datasets.

- Storage: Choosing the right storage solution (HDFS, object storage, data lakes) based on data size, access patterns, and cost.
- Compression: Reducing data size to optimize storage and processing efficiency.

Data Complexity

- Data Structures: Handling diverse data formats (structured, semi-structured, unstructured).
- Data Processing: Selecting appropriate tools and frameworks (Hadoop, Spark, SQL, NoSQL) for different data complexities.
- Data Quality: Ensuring data accuracy, consistency, and completeness for reliable analysis.
- Data Integration: Combining data from multiple sources while maintaining data integrity.

Performance Optimization Techniques

- Indexing: Creating indexes for frequently accessed data to improve query performance.
- Caching: Storing frequently used data in memory for faster access.

- Query Optimization: Analyzing and improving query performance through techniques like query rewriting and execution plans.
- Distributed Computing: Distributing workloads across multiple nodes for parallel processing.
- Hardware Acceleration: Utilizing GPUs or specialized hardware for computationally intensive tasks.

Balancing Scalability and Performance

- Trade-offs: Often, there's a trade-off between scalability and performance. Finding the right balance depends on specific requirements.
- Architecture Design: Carefully designing the data architecture to accommodate growth while maintaining performance.
- Monitoring and Optimization: Continuously monitoring system performance and making adjustments as needed.

Example: A financial institution dealing with high-frequency trading data requires a system that can handle massive data volumes in real-time with low latency. This necessitates distributed processing, in-memory caching, and specialized hardware for optimal performance.

The Complexity of Data Transformations

Data transformation is a critical step in the data lifecycle, but it can also be a complex and time-consuming process. Several factors contribute to this complexity:

Data Quality Issues

- Inconsistent data formats: Data from various sources often has different structures and formats.
- Missing values: Incomplete data can hinder analysis and modeling.
- Data inconsistencies: Errors, duplicates, and outliers can distort results.

- Data cleaning and standardization: These processes can be labor-intensive and require domain expertise.

Data Volume and Velocity

- Large datasets: Processing and transforming massive amounts of data can be computationally intensive.
- Real-time processing: Transforming data in real-time requires efficient and scalable solutions.
- Batch vs. streaming: Different approaches have different complexities and challenges.

Data Variety

- Structured, unstructured, and semi-structured data: Handling different data formats requires diverse transformation techniques.
- Data enrichment: Adding external data sources can increase complexity.
- Data normalization: Transforming data into a standard format can be challenging for complex structures.

Business Logic and Transformations

- Complex calculations: Derived metrics and calculations can be intricate.
- Data aggregations and summarizations: Transforming data into meaningful summaries requires careful consideration.
- Data transformations for specific analyses: Different analyses may require different data transformations.

Tooling and Infrastructure

- ETL/ELT tools: Selecting the right tools for the job can be challenging.

- Data integration challenges: Combining data from multiple sources can be complex.
- Scalability and performance: Ensuring transformation processes can handle increasing data volumes and complexity.

Overcoming Challenges

- Data profiling: Understanding data characteristics before transformation.
- Data quality assessment: Identifying and addressing data issues.
- Data mapping: Clearly defining how data will be transformed.
- ETL/ELT tools: Leveraging tools to automate and streamline processes.
- Incremental transformations: Processing data in smaller batches for efficiency.
- Testing and validation: Ensuring data accuracy and consistency after transformations.

By carefully addressing these complexities, organizations can improve the efficiency and effectiveness of their data transformation processes, leading to better data-driven decision making.

Key Factors for Successful Integration

- Data Formats: Compatibility in data formats, such as CSV, JSON, Parquet, or Avro, ensures smooth data transfer between systems.
- Connectors and APIs: Robust connectors and APIs facilitate data exchange and interaction between tools.
- Data Modeling: Aligning data models in the data warehouse with the BI tool's requirements is crucial for efficient analysis.
- ETL/ELT Processes: Efficient data extraction, transformation, and loading capabilities are vital for preparing data for analysis.
- Performance Optimization: Ensuring optimal performance for data retrieval and processing is essential for interactive analysis.

- Security and Governance: Maintaining data security and compliance throughout the integration process.

Popular Data Warehousing and BI Tool Combinations

- Cloud-based Solutions:
    - Amazn Redshift with Amazon QuickSight
    - Gogle BigQuery with Looker
    - Snwflake with Tableau
- On-premises Solutions:
    - Teradata with Micrstrategy
    - Oracle Data Warehuse with Oracle BI
    - Micrsoft SQL Server with Power BI

Challenges and Considerations

- Data Volume and Complexity: Handling large and complex datasets requires efficient integration and processing.
- Data Quality: Ensuring data consistency and accuracy across systems is essential.
- Performance Bottlenecks: Identifying and addressing performance issues to enable timely insights.
- Tool Limitations: Understanding the capabilities and limitations of each tool to optimize integration.
- Data Governance: Implementing data governance policies to protect data integrity and security.

Best Practices

- Data Profiling: Thoroughly understanding data characteristics before integration.

- ETL Optimization: Implementing efficient ETL processes to minimize data load times.
- Incremental Loads: Updating data in the data warehouse incrementally to improve performance.
- Data Modeling Best Practices: Designing effective data models for both data warehousing and BI tools.
- User Training: Providing training on BI tools and data exploration techniques.

By carefully considering these factors and implementing best practices, organizations can achieve seamless integration between data warehousing and BI tools, enabling data-driven insights and informed decision-making.

Cost and Licensing:

Cost and licensing are critical factors in selecting data management and analytics tools. Understanding the various licensing models and cost structures is essential for making informed decisions.

Licensing Models

- Perpetual Licenses: One-time purchase for unlimited use, but often without software updates or support.
- Subscription Licenses: Regular payments for ongoing access to software, including updates and support.
- Usage-Based Licensing: Pay based on consumption, such as the amount of data processed or storage used.
- Concurrent User Licenses: Based on the number of users accessing the software simultaneously.

Cost Considerations

- Upfront Costs: Initial investment in software, hardware, and implementation.
- Ongoing Costs: Subscription fees, maintenance, support, and cloud storage.

- Hidden Costs: Additional expenses for data storage, processing, and network bandwidth.
- Total Cost of Ownership (TCO): Evaluating the overall cost of a solution over its lifecycle.

Balancing Budget Constraints

- Prioritize Needs: Identify essential functionalities and features.
- Open-Source Alternatives: Consider free or low-cost open-source options.
- Cloud-Based Solutions: Explore cloud-based services with pay-as-you-go models.
- Cost-Benefit Analysis: Weigh the cost of a solution against its expected benefits.
- Negotiation: Explore potential discounts or licensing flexibility with vendors.

Additional Factors

- Scalability: The ability to accommodate increasing data volumes and user needs.
- Flexibility: Adaptability to changing business requirements.
- Vendor Support: The level of support provided by the vendor.
- Compliance: Adherence to industry regulations and standards.

Example: A small business with limited budget might opt for a cloud-based data warehousing solution with a subscription model, offering scalability and cost-efficiency. A large enterprise with complex data needs and stringent compliance requirements might invest in a perpetual license for an on-premises data warehouse with robust security features.

By carefully considering these factors, organizations can select the most suitable data management and analytics solutions within their budget constraints while meeting their business objectives.

Support and Community:

A robust support system and a thriving community are essential for the successful adoption and utilization of data management and analytics tools.

Types of Support

- **Vendor Support:**
  - Technical assistance for troubleshooting issues.
  - Product training and certification programs.
  - Access to knowledge bases and documentation.
  - Priority support options for critical issues.
- **Community Support:**
  - Online forums and communities for knowledge sharing and problem-solving.
  - User groups and meetups for networking and collaboration.
  - Open-source contributions and development.
- **Internal Support:**
  - Dedicated IT support teams for system administration and maintenance.
  - Data analysts and scientists for data modeling and analysis.
  - Business users with domain expertise for problem definition and interpretation.

Importance of a Strong Community

- **Knowledge Sharing:** Fostering collaboration and learning from peers.
- **Best Practices:** Sharing insights and experiences to improve implementations.
- **Problem Solving:** Accessing collective expertise to address challenges.

- **Innovation:** Driving new ideas and approaches through community engagement.

Key Considerations

- **Support Channels:** Availability of various support channels (phone, email, online chat, forums).
- **Response Time:** Speed of response to critical issues.
- **Skill Level:** Expertise of support personnel.
- **Community Size and Activity:** The vibrancy and engagement of the user community.
- **Documentation and Resources:** Availability of comprehensive documentation and learning materials.

Examples of Strong Support and Community Ecosystems

- **Open-source communities:** Apache Hadoop, Apache Spark, Python's data science ecosystem.
- **Cloud platform communities:** AWS, Azure, GCP.
- **Business intelligence tool communities:** Tableau, Power BI, Looker.

By carefully evaluating the support and community aspects of different tools and platforms, organizations can make informed decisions that minimize implementation risks and maximize the return on investment.

Best Practices for ETL

- **Data profiling:** Understand data characteristics before designing ETL processes.
- **Data quality:** Implement data cleansing and validation steps.
- **Error handling:**Build robust error handling mechanisms.
- **Performance optimization:** Optimize ETL processes for speed and efficiency.

- **Testing and validation:** Thoroughly test ETL processes before deployment.
- **Documentation:** Maintain clear and up-to-date documentation.

By carefully selecting and implementing an ETL tool, organizations can effectively extract value from their data and make informed decisions.

CHAPTER SEVEN

DATA VISUALIZATION TOOLS

Data visualization is the art of presenting data in a graphical format to make it easier to understand and interpret. It's crucial for businesses to make informed decisions and communicate insights effectively. Let's explore some popular data visualization tools:

Types of Data Visualization Tools

- **Business Intelligence (BI) and Data Analytics Platforms:** These offer comprehensive data visualization capabilities along with data integration and analysis features.
    - Examples: Tableau, Power BI, Looker, Qlik, Sisense
- **Specialized Visualization Tools:** These focus on specific types of visualizations or industries.
    - Examples: Geographic Information Systems (GIS) for maps, statistical software like R or Python for custom visualizations.
- **Embedding Visualization Libraries:** These can be integrated into web applications or custom dashboards.
    - Examples: D3.js, Chart.js, Highcharts

Key Factors to Consider

- **Ease of use:** Consider the tool's interface and learning curve.
- **Data connectivity:** Ensure compatibility with your data sources.
- **Visualization options:** Check the variety of charts, graphs, and maps available.
- **Interactivity:** Evaluate the ability to drill down and explore data.
- **Collaboration:** Consider features for sharing and collaborating on visualizations.
- **Cost:** Compare pricing models and features offered at different tiers.

Best Practices for Data Visualization

- **Choose the right chart type:** Select the chart that best represents your data and story.
- **Keep it simple:** Avoid cluttering visualizations with too much information.
- **Use color effectively:** Color can enhance data understanding but use it judiciously.
- **Label axes clearly:** Ensure clarity in data interpretation.
- **Provide context:** Explain the story behind the data.

By effectively utilizing data visualization tools and following best practices, you can unlock the potential of your data and make data-driven decisions with confidence.

Big Data Analytics Techniques

Data Mining

Data mining is the process of discovering patterns in large data sets involving methods at the intersection of machine learning, statistics, and database systems. It is an exploratory analysis

Key Techniques:

- Association rule learning: Discovering relationships between variables in large databases.

- Classification: Assigning data instances to predefined classes or categories.
- Clustering: Grouping similar data points together without predefined labels.
- Regression: Predicting continuous numerical values based on input variables.
- Anomaly detection: Identifying unusual patterns or outliers.

Machine Learning

Machine learning is a subset of artificial intelligence that provides systems the ability to automatically learn and improve from experience without being explicitly programmed. Machine learning focuses on the development of computer programs that can access data and use it to learn for themselves.

Key Techniques:

- Supervised learning: Algorithms learn from labeled data to make predictions on new, unseen data.
- Unsupervised learning: Algorithms find patterns in unlabeled data.
- Reinforcement learning: Agents learn to make decisions by interacting with an environment and receiving rewards or penalties.

Relationship Between Data Mining and Machine Learning

Data mining often employs machine learning algorithms as tools to extract knowledge from data. However, data mining is a broader field that encompasses various techniques, including statistical methods and visualization.

In essence:

- Data mining is the process of discovering patterns.
- Machine learning is a set of techniques used in data mining.

Applications

Both data mining and machine learning have a wide range of applications across industries:

- **Business:** Customer segmentation, fraud detection, market basket analysis, churn prediction.
- **Healthcare:** Disease diagnosis, drug discovery, patient data analysis.
- **Finance:** Stock price prediction, risk assessment, fraud detection.
- **Marketing:** Customer relationship management, targeted advertising, recommendation systems.

Predictive Analytics

Predictive analytics is the use of data to forecast future outcomes. It involves analyzing historical data to identify patterns and trends, which are then used to build models that predict future events or behaviors.

How Does it Work?

1. **Data Collection:** Gathering relevant historical data from various sources.
2. **Data Preparation:** Cleaning, transforming, and preparing data for analysis.
3. **Model Building:** Using statistical methods, machine learning algorithms, or a combination of both to create predictive models.
4. **Model Validation:** Testing the model's accuracy and reliability on a separate dataset.
5. **Deployment:** Integrating the model into operational systems to make predictions.

Techniques Used in Predictive Analytics

- **Regression Analysis:** Predicting numerical values (e.g., sales, prices).

- **Time Series Analysis:** Forecasting future values based on historical data.
- **Decision Trees:** Creating a tree-like model of decisions and their possible consequences.
- **Neural Networks:** Simulating the human brain to identify patterns in complex data.
- **Machine Learning Algorithms:** Various algorithms like support vector machines, random forests, and gradient boosting.

Applications of Predictive Analytics

- **Customer Relationship Management (CRM):** Customer churn prediction, customer lifetime value estimation, targeted marketing.
- **Finance:** Fraud detection, risk assessment, investment portfolio optimization.
- **Healthcare:** Disease prediction, patient risk assessment, drug discovery.
- **Retail:** Demand forecasting, inventory management, personalized recommendations.
- **Manufacturing:** Predictive maintenance, supply chain optimization.

Challenges in Predictive Analytics

- **Data Quality:** Ensuring data accuracy and completeness.
- **Model Complexity:** Building models that are interpretable and explainable.
- **Overfitting:** Creating models that are too closely fit to the training data and perform poorly on new data.
- **Ethical Considerations:** Addressing biases in data and models.

Predictive analytics has the potential to revolutionize decision-making across industries by providing insights into future trends and outcomes.

Prescriptive Analytics:

Prescriptive analytics is the pinnacle of data analysis, going beyond simply understanding what happened (descriptive) or predicting what might happen (predictive). It answers the crucial question: "What should we do?"

How Does it Work?

Prescriptive analytics leverages advanced techniques like:

- **Optimization:** Finds the best possible solution within given constraints.
- **Simulation:** Models different scenarios to assess potential outcomes.
- **Machine Learning:** Identifies patterns and trends to inform decisions.
- **Artificial Intelligence:** Emulates human intelligence to make recommendations.

By combining these methods with historical data, real-time information, and business objectives, prescriptive analytics provides actionable recommendations.

Real-world Applications

- **Supply Chain Optimization:** Determines optimal inventory levels, transportation routes, and supplier choices.
- **Financial Portfolio Management:** Recommends investment strategies based on risk tolerance and return goals.
- **Healthcare:** Suggests treatment plans, resource allocation, and patient management strategies.
- **Marketing:** Optimizes pricing, promotions, and customer segmentation for maximum ROI.
- **Manufacturing:** Improves production scheduling, quality control, and maintenance planning.

Example:

- **Optimize inventory:** Predict product demand, considering factors like weather, seasonality, and promotions.
- **Personalize recommendations:** Suggest products based on customer purchase history and preferences.
- **Price optimization:** Dynamically adjust prices based on competition, demand, and customer segments.

Benefits of Prescriptive Analytics

- **Improved decision-making:** Provides data-driven insights to support strategic choices.
- **Increased efficiency:** Optimizes operations and resource utilization.
- **Enhanced profitability:** Maximizes revenue and minimizes costs.
- **Competitive advantage:** Gain a strategic edge by making proactive decisions.

In essence, prescriptive analytics empowers organizations to move from reactive to proactive decision-making, driving significant business value.

Real-Time Analytics: Real-time analytics is the process of examining data as it's generated, providing insights and actionable information instantaneously. Unlike traditional analytics that often involves batch processing and delayed reporting, real-time analytics delivers insights in seconds or even milliseconds.

How Does it Work?

To achieve real-time analytics, organizations rely on:

- **High-speed data ingestion:** Capturing data from various sources at rapid speeds.
- **Data streaming:** Processing data as a continuous flow rather than in batches.
- **In-memory computing:** Storing data in computer memory for faster access and processing.

- **Advanced analytics algorithms:** Applying complex calculations and models on the fly.
- **Low-latency visualization:** Displaying insights in user-friendly dashboards and reports.

Benefits of Real-Time Analytics

- **Faster decision-making:** Respond to changing conditions quickly.
- **Improved customer experience:** Deliver personalized offers and support.
- **Increased efficiency:** Optimize operations and resource allocation.
- **Reduced risk:** Detect anomalies and potential issues early.
- **Competitive advantage:** Gain insights before competitors.

Real-world Applications

- **Financial Services:** Fraud detection, market trend analysis, algorithmic trading.
- **Retail:** Inventory management, personalized recommendations, customer churn prediction.
- **Manufacturing:** Predictive maintenance, quality control, supply chain optimization.
- **Healthcare:** Patient monitoring, real-time alerts, resource allocation.
- **Marketing:** Campaign performance analysis, customer segmentation, ad optimization.

Challenges of Real-Time Analytics

- **Data volume and velocity:** Handling massive amounts of data at high speed.
- **Data quality:** Ensuring data accuracy and consistency.

- **Infrastructure:** Building and maintaining a robust real-time analytics platform.
- **Talent:** Finding skilled professionals with expertise in real-time technologies.

Real-time analytics is transforming industries by enabling businesses to harness the power of the present moment.

Text Analytics and Natural Language Processing (NLP)

Text Analytics

- Text analytics, often referred to as text mining, is the process of deriving high-quality information from text.
- It involves the discovery of patterns, trends, and useful information from text. This can be applied to various types of text, including documents, emails, social media posts, and more.

Key components of text analytics:

- **Information extraction**: Identifying specific data points within text (e.g., names, dates, locations).
- **Text classification**: Categorizing text into predefined categories (e.g., spam, not spam).
- **Sentiment analysis**: Determining the sentiment expressed in text (positive, negative, neutral).
- **Topic modeling**: Identifying the main topics or themes within a collection of documents.

Natural Language Processing (NLP)

NLP is a branch of artificial intelligence that focuses on the interaction between computers and human language. It involves teaching computers to understand, interpret, and generate human language in a way that is both meaningful and useful.

Key NLP techniques:

- **Tokenization:** Breaking text into individual words or tokens.

- **Stemming and lemmatization**: Reducing words to their root form.
- **Part-of-speech tagging**: Identifying the grammatical role of words.
- **Named entity recognition**: Identifying and classifying named entities (e.g., persons, organizations, locations).
- **Dependency parsing:** Analyzing the grammatical structure of sentences.
- **Machine translation**: Translating text from one language to another.
- **Text summarization**: Creating concise summaries of longer texts.

Relationship Between Text Analytics and NLP

NLP techniques are fundamental to text analytics. They provide the tools to preprocess and understand text data before applying analytical methods. In essence, NLP is the foundation upon which text analytics is built.

Applications

Text analytics and NLP have a wide range of applications across various industries, including:

Customer service: Analyzing customer feedback to identify trends and improve service.

Understanding the power of customer feedback is crucial for businesses looking to enhance their customer service. By systematically analyzing feedback, organizations can identify recurring issues, pinpoint areas for improvement, and ultimately deliver exceptional customer experiences.

Key Steps in Analyzing Customer Feedback

1. **Data Collection:**

    - Gather feedback from various channels: surveys, emails, social media, reviews, call center interactions, and customer support tickets.

- Ensure data consistency and accuracy for effective analysis.

2. **Data Organization:**
   - Categorize feedback into relevant themes or topics (e.g., product quality, customer service, delivery, pricing).
   - Use tagging or labeling systems to identify key points within each piece of feedback.
3. **Sentiment Analysis:**
   - Determine the overall sentiment of the feedback (positive, negative, neutral).
   - Utilize sentiment analysis tools to process large volumes of text efficiently.
4. **Trend Identification:**
   - Look for patterns and recurring issues across different feedback sources.
   - Analyze feedback over time to identify emerging trends or changes in customer sentiment.
5. **Prioritization:**
   - Determine the impact of identified issues on customer satisfaction and business performance.
   - Prioritize areas for improvement based on their severity and potential impact.
6. **Action Planning:**
   - Develop specific action plans to address identified issues.
   - Assign responsibilities and set deadlines for implementation.

7. **Performance Measurement:**

    - Track the effectiveness of implemented changes by monitoring customer satisfaction metrics.
    - Continuously analyze feedback to measure progress and identify new areas for improvement.

Risk management: Detecting potential risks or threats in textual data (e.g., news articles, financial reports).

Textual data is a rich source of information that can be leveraged to identify potential risks and threats. By applying advanced techniques, organizations can extract valuable insights and make informed decisions.

Key Techniques and Applications

- **Natural Language Processing (NLP):**

    - **Entity Recognition:** Identify key entities like people, organizations, locations, and products to understand the context of the text.
    - **Sentiment Analysis:** Determine the overall sentiment expressed in the text (positive, negative, neutral) to gauge potential risks.
    - **Keyword Extraction:** Extract relevant keywords to identify topics and potential threats.

- **Machine Learning:**

    - **Anomaly Detection:** Identify unusual patterns or outliers in the text that may indicate potential risks.
    - **Classification:** Categorize text into predefined risk categories (e.g., financial, reputational, operational).
    - **Predictive Modeling:** Build models to predict the likelihood of specific risks based on textual data.

- **Risk Categories:**
  - **Financial Risks:** Identify indicators of financial instability, fraud, or market fluctuations.
  - **Reputational Risks:** Detect potential threats to brand image, customer trust, or public perception.
  - **Operational Risks:** Identify potential disruptions to business operations, supply chain issues, or regulatory compliance problems.
  - **Strategic Risks:** Detect emerging trends, competitive threats, or changes in market dynamics.

Example Use Cases

- **Financial Services:**
  - Detect early warning signs of financial distress in news articles and financial reports.
  - Identify potential fraud or money laundering activities through transaction data analysis.
  - Monitor market sentiment and assess investment risks.
- **Healthcare:**
  - Identify potential drug safety issues or adverse events from medical literature and social media.
  - Monitor public health crises and outbreaks through news and social media data.
- **Government:**
  - Detect potential threats to national security or public safety through news and social media monitoring.
  - Analyze public opinion on government policies and identify potential risks to political stability.

Legal: Analyzing legal documents for key information and insights.

Legal documents are often complex and voluminous, making it challenging to extract crucial information efficiently.

Fortunately, advancements in technology, particularly in the realm of Natural Language Processing (NLP), have revolutionized how legal professionals approach document analysis.

Key Techniques and Applications

- **Information Extraction:**
  - Identifying and extracting specific data points like names, dates, amounts, and clauses.
  - Identifying key entities like parties, organizations, and locations.
- **Document Summarization:**
  - Generating concise summaries of lengthy legal documents to expedite review.
- **Contract Analysis:**
  - Identifying key clauses, obligations, and potential risks within contracts.
  - Comparing contracts to identify discrepancies or inconsistencies.
- **Due Diligence:**
  - Analyzing large volumes of documents to identify potential risks and liabilities.
  - Extracting relevant information for financial analysis and valuation.

- **Legal Research:**
  - Identifying relevant case law and statutes based on specific legal queries.
  - Analyzing case precedents to predict case outcomes.

CHAPTER EIGHT

BEST PRACTICES FOR BIG DATA ANALYTICS

Data Governance

Data governance is the overall management of the availability, usability, integrity, and security of the data within an enterprise. It's about ensuring that data is aligned with the organization's goals and strategies.

Key components of data governance:

- **Data definition and standards**: Establishing clear definitions and standards for data elements.
- **Data ownership and stewardship**: Assigning responsibility for data management.
- **Data quality**: Ensuring data is accurate, complete, consistent, and relevant.
- **Data security and privacy**: Protecting data from unauthorized access and misuse.
- **Data retention and disposal**: Managing data lifecycle and compliance with regulations.

Data Quality

Data quality refers to the accuracy, completeness, consistency, and timeliness of data. It's about ensuring that data is fit for its intended use.

Key dimensions of data quality:

- **Accuracy**: Data is correct and free from errors.
- **Completeness**: Data is complete and contains all necessary information.
- **Consistency**: Data is consistent across different sources and formats.
- **Timeliness**: Data is up-to-date and relevant.
- **Validity**: Data conforms to defined business rules and constraints.
- **Uniqueness**: Data is free from duplicates.

Relationship Between Data Governance and Data Quality

Data governance provides the framework for achieving and maintaining data quality. A strong data governance program is essential for ensuring that data is managed effectively and meets the needs of the organization.

Challenges in Data Governance and Quality

- **Data silos**: Data scattered across different systems and departments.
- **Data quality issues**: Inaccurate, incomplete, or inconsistent data.
- **Lack of data ownership**: Unclear responsibilities for data management.
- **Regulatory compliance**: Meeting complex data privacy and security requirements.
- **Data volume and variety**: Managing increasing amounts of data in different formats.

Best Practices for Data Governance and Quality

- Establish a data governance framework: Define roles, responsibilities, and processes.
- Implement data quality management programs: Define data quality metrics and standards.

- Use data profiling and cleansing tools: Identify and correct data issues.
- Foster a data-driven culture: Encourage data-informed decision-making.
- Continuously monitor and improve data quality: Track data quality metrics and take corrective actions.

Data Security and Privacy

Data security and privacy are two critical aspects of managing information in today's digital age. While often used interchangeably, they have distinct meanings.

Data Security

Data security focuses on protecting data from unauthorized access, use, disclosure, disruption, modification, or destruction. It's about safeguarding the integrity, availability, and confidentiality of data.

Key components of data security:

- **Access control:** Limiting access to data based on user roles and permissions.
- **Encryption:** Converting data into a code to prevent unauthorized access.
- **Network security:** Protecting the network infrastructure from cyberattacks.
- **Data loss prevention (DLP):** Preventing sensitive data from leaving the organization.
- **Incident response:** Having a plan in place to respond to data breaches.

Data Privacy

Data privacy is about protecting individual rights and controlling the collection, storage, use, and disclosure of personal information. It's about ensuring that data is handled ethically and responsibly.

Key components of data privacy:

- **Data minimization:** Collecting only the necessary data.
- **Data retention:** Determining how long data is kept.
- **Data subject rights:** Providing individuals with control over their data.
- **Privacy by design:** Incorporating privacy considerations into system development.
- **Compliance:** Adhering to data protection regulations (e.g., GDPR, CCPA).

Relationship Between Data Security and Privacy

Data security is a prerequisite for data privacy. Strong security measures are essential to protect personal information from unauthorized access, which is a fundamental aspect of data privacy. However, data privacy goes beyond security by addressing the ethical and legal implications of data handling.

Challenges in Data Security and Privacy

- **Evolving threats:** New cyber threats emerge constantly.
- **Data breaches:** High-profile data breaches erode trust.
- **Regulatory compliance:** Meeting complex and changing data protection laws.
- **Data volume:** Managing large amounts of data increases risks.
- **Employee awareness:** Ensuring employees understand security and privacy best practices.

Best Practices for Data Security and Privacy

- **Risk assessment:** Identify and prioritize potential threats.
- **Employee training:** Educate employees about security and privacy.
- **Incident response planning:** Develop a plan to respond to data breaches.
- **Data encryption:** Protect data both at rest and in transit.
- **Regular security audits:** Assess vulnerabilities and implement improvements.

- **Privacy by design:** Incorporate privacy into system development.

Big Data Project Management

Big Data projects present unique challenges due to their scale, complexity, and velocity. Effective project management is crucial for success.

Challenges in Big Data Project Management

- **Data Volume:** Handling massive datasets requires efficient storage and processing solutions.
- **Data Variety:** Dealing with structured, unstructured, and semi-structured data necessitates diverse tools and techniques.
- **Data Velocity:** Processing real-time data demands high-performance infrastructure and analytics.
- **Data Veracity:** Ensuring data quality and accuracy is essential for reliable insights.
- **Talent Scarcity:** Finding skilled professionals with Big Data expertise can be challenging.
- **Infrastructure Complexity:** Building and maintaining a robust Big Data infrastructure is costly and time-consuming.

Key Considerations for Big Data Project Management

- **Clear Project Objectives:** Define specific goals and expected outcomes.
- **Data Strategy:** Develop a comprehensive data strategy, including data acquisition, storage, processing, and analysis.
- **Technology Selection:** Choose appropriate Big Data technologies (Hadoop, Spark, etc.) based on project requirements.
- **Data Governance:** Establish data quality standards, ownership, and access controls.
- **Talent Management:** Build a skilled team with diverse expertise.

- **Risk Management:** Identify potential risks and develop mitigation strategies.
- **Change Management:** Effectively manage changes in project scope, technology, or business requirements.
- **Agile Methodology:** Consider using agile frameworks to adapt to changing project needs.

Roles and Responsibilities

- **Project Manager:** Oversees the entire project, from initiation to closure.
- **Data Architect:** Designs the data infrastructure and architecture.
- **Data Engineer:** Builds and maintains the Big Data platform.
- **Data Scientist:** Extracts insights and value from the data.
- **Data Analyst:** Prepares and analyzes data for reporting and visualization.

Tools and Technologies

- **Hadoop:** For storing and processing large datasets.
- **Spark:** For real-time data processing and machine learning.
- **NoSQL Databases:** For handling unstructured and semi-structured data.
- **Cloud Platforms:** For scalable and cost-effective infrastructure (AWS, Azure, GCP).
- **Data Visualization Tools:** For presenting insights effectively (Tableau, Power BI).

Best Practices

- **Start Small:** Begin with a pilot project to test the approach.
- **Iterative Development:** Embrace an iterative process to refine the solution.

- **Continuous Monitoring:** Track project performance and make adjustments as needed.
- **Collaboration:** Foster collaboration among team members and stakeholders.
- **Data Quality Focus:** Prioritize data quality throughout the project.

By following these guidelines and leveraging the right tools and technologies, organizations can successfully manage Big Data projects and unlock valuable insights.

Ethical Considerations in Big Data

The power of big data comes with significant ethical responsibilities. As organizations collect and analyze vast amounts of data, they must navigate complex issues related to privacy, bias, transparency, and accountability.

Key Ethical Concerns

- **Privacy:**
    - Data collection without explicit consent
    - Over-collection of personal information
    - Data breaches and unauthorized access
- **Bias:**
    - Algorithmic bias leading to discriminatory outcomes
    - Reinforcing existing societal inequalities
    - Unfair targeting of specific groups
- **Transparency:**
    - Lack of clarity about data collection and usage
    - Black box algorithms and decision-making processes
    - Misleading data visualizations

- **Accountability:**
    - Responsibility for data-driven decisions and their consequences
    - Liability for data breaches and privacy violations

Ethical Frameworks and Guidelines

To address these challenges, organizations should adopt ethical frameworks and guidelines such as:

- **Privacy by Design:** Incorporating privacy considerations from the outset of data projects.
- **Fairness and Accountability:** Ensuring algorithms and models are unbiased and transparent.
- **Data Minimization:** Collecting only necessary data and securely storing it.
- **Data Subject Rights:** Empowering individuals to control their data.
- **Ethical Impact Assessments:** Evaluating the potential ethical implications of data projects.

Best Practices

- **Transparency:** Be open about data collection, usage, and sharing practices.
- **Consent:** Obtain explicit and informed consent from data subjects.
- **Data Quality:** Ensure data accuracy, completeness, and consistency.
- **Bias Mitigation:** Identify and address biases in data and algorithms.
- **Privacy Protection:** Implement robust security measures to protect data.
- **Ethical Review:** Conduct regular ethical assessments of data practices.

By prioritizing ethical considerations, organizations can build trust with stakeholders, mitigate risks, and contribute to a positive societal impact.

Return on Investment (ROI) Measurement

Return on Investment (ROI) is a performance measure used to evaluate the efficiency of an investment or to compare the efficiency of a number of different investments.

ROI is calculated by subtracting the cost of an investment from its final value, dividing this new number by the investment's cost, and then multiplying it by 100.

ROI Formula

- ROI = [(Profit - Cost of Investment) / Cost of Investment] * 100

Key Components of ROI

- **Profit:** The net gain from the investment.
- **Cost of Investment:** The initial outlay of funds.

Challenges in Calculating ROI

- **Defining Profit:** Determining the exact profit can be complex, especially for long-term investments or intangible benefits.
- **Calculating Cost of Investment:** Including all associated costs (e.g., opportunity cost, overhead) can be challenging.
- **Time Value of Money:** ROI doesn't consider the time value of money, making it less accurate for long-term investments.

Improving ROI Measurement

- **Clearly Define Goals:** Establish specific, measurable, achievable, relevant, and time-bound (SMART) goals.
- **Identify Key Performance Indicators (KPIs):** Determine the metrics that directly correlate with ROI.

- **Consider Time Value of Money:** Use metrics like Net Present Value (NPV) or Internal Rate of Return (IRR) for long-term investments.
- **Include Intangible Benefits:** Quantify the impact of intangible benefits (e.g., brand reputation, customer satisfaction) whenever possible.
- **Compare to Benchmarks:** Evaluate ROI against industry standards or similar investments.

ROI in Different Contexts

- **Financial Investments:** Stocks, bonds, real estate.
- **Marketing Campaigns:** Advertising, promotions, social media.
- **Business Projects:** New product launches, process improvements.
- **Human Capital:** Employee training, development programs.

Limitations of ROI

- **Focus on Financial Returns:** Doesn't consider non-financial benefits like customer satisfaction or employee morale.
- **Rear-View Mirror:** Measures past performance, not future potential.
- **Sensitivity to Data Accuracy:** Inaccurate data can lead to misleading ROI calculations.

CHAPTER NINE

CASE STUIDIES AND INDUSTRY APPLICATIONS

Big Data in Finance:

Big data has revolutionized the financial industry, enabling institutions to make data-driven decisions, identify new opportunities, and manage risks more effectively.

How Big Data is Used in Finance:

- **Risk Management:**
    - Identifying potential risks through pattern recognition in vast datasets.
    - Early detection of fraudulent activities.
    - Assessing creditworthiness of borrowers.
- **Trading:**
    - High-frequency trading (HFT) based on real-time market data analysis.
    - Algorithmic trading to automate trading decisions.
    - Predictive modeling for market trends.

- **Customer Relationship Management (CRM):**
    - Personalized financial products and services based on customer behavior.
    - Customer segmentation for targeted marketing campaigns.
    - Fraud detection and prevention.
- **Fraud Detection:**
    - Identifying unusual patterns in transaction data.
    - Real-time fraud detection and prevention.
    - Building robust fraud prevention models.
- **Investment Analysis:**
    - Analyzing market trends and investor sentiment.
    - Portfolio optimization based on risk and return profiles.
    - Identifying investment opportunities.

Challenges and Opportunities

While big data offers immense potential, financial institutions face challenges such as:

- **Data Quality:** Ensuring data accuracy and consistency.
- **Data Security:** Protecting sensitive financial data from breaches.
- **Talent Acquisition:** Finding skilled data scientists and analysts.
- **Infrastructure:** Building and maintaining a robust big data infrastructure.

However, these challenges also present opportunities for innovation and competitive advantage.

Examples of Big Data Applications in Finance

- **Credit Scoring:** Using alternative data sources (social media, online behavior) to assess creditworthiness.

- **Insurance:** Analyzing customer data to develop personalized insurance products and pricing.
- **Wealth Management:** Providing tailored investment advice based on individual investor profiles.

Big Data in Healthcare:

Big data is transforming the healthcare industry by enabling better patient care, improved operational efficiency, and the discovery of new treatments.

Applications of Big Data in Healthcare:

- **Precision Medicine**: Analyzing genetic data, electronic health records (EHRs), and other patient information to tailor treatments to individual patients.
- **Disease Prevention**: Identifying risk factors and predicting disease outbreaks through data analysis.
- **Drug Discovery**: Accelerating drug development by analyzing vast amounts of molecular data.
- **Clinical Trials**: Optimizing patient recruitment and trial design.
- **Fraud Detection**: Identifying fraudulent claims and suspicious patterns in healthcare spending.
- **Patient Outcomes**: Measuring the effectiveness of treatments and identifying areas for improvement.
- **Supply Chain Management**: Optimizing inventory levels and reducing costs.

Challenges and Opportunities

While big data holds immense promise, healthcare organizations face challenges such as:

- **Data Quality**: Ensuring data accuracy, completeness, and consistency.
- **Data Privacy**: Protecting sensitive patient information.
- **Interoperability**: Integrating data from different systems and formats.

- **Data Security**: Safeguarding data from cyberattacks.

However, these challenges also present opportunities for innovation and competitive advantage.

Examples of Big Data in Action

- **Wearable Devices**: Analyzing data from wearables to monitor patient health and detect early signs of disease.
- **Telemedicine**: Using big data to improve remote patient monitoring and virtual consultations.
- **Population Health Management**: Identifying health trends and disparities within populations.

Big Data in Marketing:

Big data has transformed the marketing landscape, enabling businesses to make data-driven decisions, understand customer behavior in unprecedented detail, and optimize marketing campaigns for maximum impact.

Key Applications of Big Data in Marketing

- **Customer Segmentation:** Creating detailed customer profiles based on demographics, purchase history, online behavior, and other relevant data to tailor marketing messages.
- **Personalized Marketing:** Delivering customized product recommendations, offers, and content based on individual preferences and behavior.
- **Customer Acquisition:** Identifying potential customers through data analysis and developing targeted acquisition strategies.
- **Customer Retention:**Analyzing customer behavior to identify churn risks and implementing retention strategies.
- **Market Research:** Gathering insights into market trends, consumer preferences, and competitor activities.
- **Campaign Optimization:** Measuring the effectiveness of marketing campaigns and allocating resources accordingly.

- **Predictive Analytics:** Forecasting customer behavior, sales trends, and market conditions.

Challenges and Opportunities

While big data offers immense potential, marketers face challenges such as:

- **Data Quality:** Ensuring data accuracy, completeness, and consistency.
- **Data Privacy:** Adhering to data protection regulations.
- **Data Security:** Protecting sensitive customer data.
- **Talent Acquisition:** Finding skilled data analysts and scientists.

Despite these challenges, big data presents significant opportunities for marketers to improve ROI, enhance customer satisfaction, and gain a competitive advantage.

Big Data in Government:

Big data is revolutionizing the way governments operate, enabling them to deliver more efficient, effective, and citizen-centric services.

Key Applications of Big Data in Government

Improved Service Delivery:

- Analyzing citizen interactions to identify service gaps and improve delivery.
- Optimizing resource allocation based on real-time data.
- Personalizing government services to meet individual needs.

Enhanced Decision Making:

- Supporting evidence-based policymaking through data-driven insights.
- Identifying trends and patterns in complex datasets.
- Predicting future needs and challenges.

Fraud Detection and Prevention:

- Detecting fraudulent activities in government programs and services.
- Protecting taxpayer funds through data analysis.

Disaster Management:

- Improving emergency response and recovery efforts through real-time data analysis.
- Allocating resources effectively during crises.

Public Safety:

- Analyzing crime data to identify patterns and hotspots.
- Optimizing police patrols and resource allocation.

Economic Development:

- Identifying economic trends and opportunities.
- Supporting business growth and job creation.

Challenges and Opportunities

While big data offers immense potential, governments face challenges such as:

- **Data Quality**: Ensuring data accuracy, completeness, and consistency.
- **Data Privacy**: Protecting sensitive citizen information.
- **Data Security**: Safeguarding government data from cyberattacks.
- **Talent Acquisition**: Finding skilled data analysts and scientists.

Despite these challenges, big data presents significant opportunities for governments to improve efficiency, transparency, and citizen satisfaction.

CHAPTER TEN

FUTURE OF BIG DATA ANALYTICS

Emerging Technologies: AI, IoT, and Blockchain

These three technologies are reshaping industries and our daily lives. Let's explore each briefly.

Artificial Intelligence (AI)

AI refers to the simulation of human intelligence in machines that are programmed to think like humans and mimic their actions.

- **Key areas:** Machine learning, natural language processing, computer vision
- **Applications:** Self-driving cars, medical diagnosis, financial trading, customer service chatbots

Internet of Things (IoT)

IoT describes the network of physical devices, vehicles, home appliances, and other items embedded with electronics, software, sensors, actuators, and connectivity which enables these objects to connect and exchange data.

- **Key components:** Sensors, connectivity, data processing
- **Applications:** Smart homes, wearables, industrial automation, supply chain management

Blockchain

Blockchain is a distributed ledger technology that records transactions across multiple computers. It is secure, transparent, and resistant to modification.

- **Key features:** Decentralization, security, transparency
- **Applications:** Cryptocurrencies, supply chain management, healthcare, voting systems

Convergence of Technologies

The real power lies in the convergence of these technologies. For example:

- **AI and IoT:** AI can analyze data from IoT devices to optimize operations, predict maintenance, and create new services.
- **Blockchain and IoT:** Blockchain can secure data generated by IoT devices and create trust in IoT ecosystems.
- **AI and Blockchain:** AI can analyze blockchain data to identify patterns, trends, and anomalies.

The rapid advancement of AI, IoT, and blockchain has brought forth a host of ethical dilemmas.

AI Ethics

- **Bias**: AI systems can perpetuate societal biases if trained on biased data.
- **Autonomy**: The development of autonomous systems raises questions about accountability and liability.
- **Job Displacement**: Automation could lead to significant job losses, requiring social safety nets and retraining programs.
- **Privacy**: AI systems can collect and analyze vast amounts of personal data, raising privacy concerns.

IoT Ethics

- **Privacy**: IoT devices collect data, potentially infringing on individual privacy.
- **Security**: IoT devices can be vulnerable to hacking, leading to data breaches and physical harm.
- **Dependency**: Overreliance on IoT devices can create vulnerabilities if systems fail.

Blockchain Ethics

- **Energy Consumption**: Some blockchain systems, particularly those based on proof-of-work, consume vast amounts of energy.
- **Privacy**: While blockchain offers transparency, it can also compromise privacy if data is not handled carefully.
- **Inequality**: The distribution of wealth generated by blockchain-based cryptocurrencies can be uneven.

Overarching Ethical Concerns

- **Accountability**: Determining responsibility for actions taken by AI systems or IoT devices.
- **Transparency**: Ensuring that the workings of AI and blockchain systems are understandable.
- **Equity**: Ensuring that benefits and risks of these technologies are distributed fairly.
- **Human Dignity**: Protecting human values and rights in an increasingly technology-driven world.

Addressing these ethical challenges requires a multidisciplinary approach involving technologists, policymakers, ethicists, and society as a whole.

Talent Development and Skillset Requirements

Talent Development

Talent development is a strategic approach to identifying, nurturing, and optimizing the potential of employees to meet current and future organizational needs. It involves a combination of training, development, and performance management to foster a high-performance culture.

Key components of talent development:

- **Needs Assessment:** Identifying skill gaps and development opportunities.
- **Learning and Development Programs:** Designing and implementing training programs.
- **Performance Management:** Setting clear expectations, providing feedback, and recognizing achievements.
- **Career Development:** Assisting employees in planning and achieving their career goals.
- **Succession Planning:** Identifying and developing high-potential employees for leadership roles.

Skillset Requirements for Talent Development Professionals

A successful talent development professional requires a blend of both hard and soft skills:

Hard Skills:

- **Learning and Development:** Curriculum design, instructional design, training delivery.
- **Performance Management:** Performance appraisal, goal setting, coaching.
- **HR Analytics:** Data analysis, metrics, reporting.
- **Change Management:** Organizational change, communication, resistance management.
- **Technology:** Learning management systems, HRIS, talent management platforms.

Soft Skills:

- **Communication:** Effective verbal and written communication.
- **Interpersonal Skills:** Building relationships, collaboration, teamwork.

- **Problem-solving:** Identifying and resolving issues.
- **Leadership:** Inspiring and motivating others.
- **Coaching and Mentoring:** Providing guidance and support.

Emerging Trends in Talent Development

- **Digital Learning:** Leveraging technology for online and mobile learning.
- **Personalized Learning:** Tailoring development experiences to individual needs.
- **Continuous Learning:** Fostering a culture of lifelong learning.
- **Employee Experience:** Creating engaging and rewarding development opportunities.
- **Data-Driven Talent Management:** Using analytics to inform talent decisions.

Big Data for Small and Medium Enterprises (SMEs)

- While often associated with large corporations, big data can be a powerful tool for SMEs to gain a competitive edge.
- By harnessing the power of data, SMEs can make informed decisions, improve efficiency, and enhance customer satisfaction.

Challenges and Opportunities for SMEs

SMEs face unique challenges when implementing big data solutions:

- **Limited resources**: Smaller budgets and fewer IT personnel.
- **Data quality**: Ensuring data accuracy and consistency.
- **Lack of expertise**: Finding skilled data analysts.

However, the potential benefits are significant:

- **Improved customer understanding**: Gain deeper insights into customer behavior and preferences.
- **Enhanced operational efficiency**: Optimize processes and reduce costs.
- **Increased revenue**: Identify new market opportunities and increase sales.
- **Competitive advantage**: Outperform larger competitors through data-driven decisions.

Mastering Big Data Analytics

- **Customer Relationship Management (CRM)**: Analyze customer data to identify high-value customers, predict churn, and personalize marketing campaigns.
- **Inventory Management**: Optimize stock levels, reduce stockouts, and improve supply chain efficiency.
- **Marketing and Sales**: Identify target markets, measure campaign effectiveness, and optimize marketing spend.
- **Financial Management**: Analyze financial data to identify trends, improve cash flow, and reduce costs.
- **Operational Efficiency**: Optimize production processes, reduce waste, and improve employee productivity.

Leveraging Cloud-Based Solutions

Cloud computing has made big data more accessible to SMEs. Cloud-based platforms offer:

- **Scalability**: The ability to handle increasing data volumes.
- **Cost-effectiveness**: Pay-as-you-go pricing models.
- **Accessibility**: User-friendly interfaces and pre-built analytics tools.

By utilizing cloud-based big data solutions, SMEs can overcome resource constraints and focus on deriving value from their data.

Open Source vs. Proprietary Tools

The choice between open-source and proprietary tools often hinges on a variety of factors, including cost, control, customization, support, and security. Let's delve into the key differences:

Open-Source Tools

Definition: Software with publicly accessible source code, allowing for modification and redistribution.

Advantages:

- **Cost-effective**: Often free to use.
- **Flexibility:** Customizable to specific needs.
- **Community-driven**: Benefits from collective knowledge and innovation.
- **Transparency**: Code is open to scrutiny for security and reliability.

Disadvantages:

- **Potential lack of support**: Reliance on community support.
- **Security risks**: Open code can be exploited.
- **Complexity**: May require technical expertise to implement and maintain.

Proprietary Tools

Definition: Software with source code owned and protected by a company.

Advantages:

- **Comprehensive support**: Vendor-provided assistance.
- **Regular updates**: Continuous improvement and security patches.
- **User-friendly interface**: Often designed for ease of use.
- **Integration:** Seamlessly integrates with other proprietary tools.

Disadvantages:

- **Higher costs**: Licensing fees and potential maintenance charges.
- **Vendor lock-in**: Dependence on the vendor for updates and support.
- **Limited customization**: Restricted modifications.

Choosing the Right Tool

The optimal choice depends on specific requirements:

- **Cost:** Open-source is generally cheaper, but consider total cost of ownership, including support and customization.
- **Control:** Open-source offers greater control over the software, while proprietary provides more vendor support.
- **Customization**: Open-source is highly customizable, but proprietary tools might offer pre-built integrations.
- **Security:** Both open-source and proprietary tools can be secure, but open-source benefits from community scrutiny.
- **Support:** Proprietary tools typically offer better support, but open-source communities provide valuable resources.
- **Hybrid Approach**: Many organizations combine open-source and proprietary tools to leverage the strengths of both. For example, using an open-source database with a proprietary analytics tool.

Big Data Analytics for Data Scientists

Big data analytics is the cornerstone of a data scientist's role. It involves extracting meaningful insights from massive and complex datasets. Let's delve into the key aspects:

Core Concepts

- **Data Volume:** Handling petabytes or even exabytes of data.
- **Data Variety:** Dealing with structured, unstructured, and semi-structured data.
- **Data Velocity:** Processing data in real-time or near real-time.
- **Data Veracity:** Ensuring data quality and reliability.

Essential Skills

- **Programming Proficiency:** Languages like Python, R, Scala for data manipulation and analysis.
- **Distributed Computing:** Understanding frameworks like Hadoop, Spark for processing large datasets.
- **Database Management:** Knowledge of SQL and NoSQL databases.
- **Machine Learning:** Applying algorithms to extract patterns from data.
- **Data Visualization:** Creating meaningful visualizations to communicate insights.
- **Statistical Analysis:** Employing statistical methods for data interpretation.
- **Domain Knowledge:** Understanding the context of the data to derive relevant insights.

Challenges and Solutions

- **Data Quality:** Implement robust data cleaning and preprocessing techniques.
- **Scalability:** Utilize cloud-based platforms and distributed computing frameworks.
- **Complexity:** Employ advanced machine learning algorithms and feature engineering.
- **Talent Scarcity:** Build strong data science teams and invest in training.

Real-World Applications

- **Fraud Detection:** Identifying anomalous patterns in financial transactions.
- **Customer Analytics:** Understanding customer behavior for personalized marketing.

- **Risk Assessment:** Evaluating potential risks in finance, insurance, and healthcare.
- **Predictive Modeling:** Forecasting trends and outcomes.
- **Recommendation Systems:** Suggesting products or services based on user preferences.

Tools and Technologies

- **Hadoop:** For storing and processing large datasets.
- **Spark:** For real-time data processing and machine learning.
- **Python Libraries:** NumPy, Pandas, Scikit-learn, TensorFlow, PyTorch.
- **R Packages:** dplyr, ggplot2, caret.
- **Cloud Platforms:** AWS, Azure, GCP.

The Future of Big Data Analytics

- **AI Integration:** Combining big data with AI for advanced insights.
- **Real-Time Analytics:** Processing data as it is generated.
- **Edge Computing:** Analyzing data closer to the data source.
- **Explainable AI:** Understanding the reasoning behind AI models.

Big Data Analytics for Business Analysts

Business analysts play a pivotal role in bridging the gap between data and business strategy. Big data analytics empowers them to extract actionable insights that drive informed decision-making.

Core Skills for Business Analysts

- **Business Acumen:** Understanding the business context and strategic objectives.
- **Data Literacy:** Familiarity with data concepts, sources, and quality.
- **Analytical Thinking:** Ability to identify patterns, trends, and correlations.

- **Storytelling:** Communicating complex insights in a clear and compelling manner.
- **Data Visualization:** Creating visual representations of data to facilitate understanding.
- **Problem-Solving:** Identifying business problems and proposing data-driven solutions.

Role of Business Analysts in Big Data Projects

- **Defining Business Requirements:** Clearly articulating the business problem and desired outcomes.
- **Data Collaboration:** Working with data scientists and engineers to access and prepare data.
- **Data Analysis:** Conducting exploratory data analysis and generating insights.
- **Business Impact Assessment:** Evaluating the potential impact of data-driven solutions.
- **Change Management:** Communicating insights and recommendations to stakeholders.

Tools and Techniques

- **Data Visualization Tools:** Tableau, Power BI, Looker
- **Data Analysis Tools:** Excel, SQL, Python, R
- **Business Intelligence Platforms:** SAP BusinessObjects, Oracle BI
- **Statistical Analysis Techniques:** Descriptive statistics, correlation analysis, hypothesis testing

Challenges and Opportunities

Data Quality: The Foundation of Trustworthy Insights

Data quality refers to the degree to which data meets the needs of the users for which it is intended. It encompasses various attributes like accuracy, completeness, consistency, timeliness, relevance, and validity.

Key Dimensions of Data Quality

- **Accuracy:** Data is correct and free from errors.
- **Completeness:** All necessary data elements are present.
- **Consistency:** Data is consistent across different sources and formats.
- **Timeliness:** Data is up-to-date and relevant.
- **Relevance:** Data is pertinent to the specific task or analysis.
- **Validity:** Data conforms to defined business rules and constraints.

Challenges in Data Quality

- **Data Entry Errors:** Human errors during data input.
- **Data Integration Issues:** Inconsistencies when combining data from multiple sources.
- **Data Loss or Corruption:** Accidental or intentional data damage.
- **Data Aging:** Outdated data becomes less relevant over time.
- **Master Data Management Challenges:** Maintaining consistency across multiple systems.

Ensuring Data Quality

- **Data Profiling:** Analyzing data to identify inconsistencies and anomalies.
- **Data Cleansing:** Correcting errors and inconsistencies.
- **Data Standardization:** Enforcing consistent data formats and definitions.
- **Data Validation:** Implementing rules to check data accuracy and completeness.
- **Data Monitoring:** Continuously monitoring data quality metrics.
- **Data Governance:** Establishing policies and procedures for data management.

Impact of Poor Data Quality

- **Incorrect Decisions:** Based on inaccurate or incomplete data.
- **Lost Revenue:** Due to errors in pricing, invoicing, or customer data.
- **Damaged Reputation:** Caused by data breaches or privacy violations.
- **Increased Costs:** Due to rework and data remediation efforts.

By prioritizing data quality, organizations can enhance decision-making, improve operational efficiency, and build trust in their data-driven initiatives.

Data Volume:

Handling large datasets efficiently is a critical aspect of modern data management. The sheer volume of data generated can overwhelm traditional data processing methods. Here are some key strategies to address this challenge:

Storage and Processing Technologies

- **Distributed File Systems:** HDFS, Apache Spark, and cloud storage solutions distribute data across multiple nodes for parallel processing.
- **Columnar Storage:** Formats like Apache Parquet or Apache ORC store data column-wise, improving query performance for analytical workloads.
- **Data Compression:** Reducing data size through compression techniques (e.g., gzip, deflate) to optimize storage and processing.
- **Data Partitioning:** Dividing large datasets into smaller, manageable chunks for parallel processing.

Processing Frameworks and Tools

- **Big Data Processing Frameworks:** Apache Spark, Hadoop MapReduce, and Apache Flink for handling large-scale data processing.

- **Data Warehousing and Data Lakes:** Storing and processing structured and unstructured data respectively.
- **In-Memory Computing:** Utilizing tools like Apache Spark for fast data processing in memory.

Optimization Techniques

- **Data Sampling:** Analyzing a representative subset of data for exploratory analysis and testing.
- **Data Reduction:** Techniques like aggregation, summarization, and dimensionality reduction to reduce data size.
- **Query Optimization:** Efficiently writing and executing queries to minimize resource consumption.
- **Indexing:** Creating indexes on frequently accessed columns to improve query performance.
- **Caching:** Storing frequently accessed data in memory for faster retrieval.

Challenges and Considerations

- **Scalability:** Ensuring the ability to handle increasing data volumes over time.
- **Performance:** Maintaining acceptable query response times.
- **Cost:** Managing storage and processing costs effectively.
- **Data Quality:** Ensuring data accuracy and consistency in large datasets.

By combining these strategies and technologies, organizations can effectively manage and derive value from large datasets.

Data Variety:

Data variety refers to the different forms data can take, broadly categorized into:

Structured Data

- Organized in a predefined format with a clear schema.
- Easily searchable and analyzable.
- Typically stored in relational databases.
- Examples: Customer records, financial data, sales figures.

Unstructured Data

- Lacks a predefined data model.
- Difficult to search and analyze without preprocessing.
- Often stored in data lakes or object storage.
- Examples: Text documents, images, videos, audio files, social media posts.

Semi-Structured Data

- Falls between structured and unstructured.
- Has some organizational properties but not a rigid schema.
- Examples: JSON, XML, CSV files.

Challenges in Handling Data Variety

- **Storage:** Requires different storage solutions for different data types.
- **Processing:** Demands diverse processing techniques and tools.
- **Analysis:** Needs various analytical approaches to extract insights.
- **Integration:** Combining structured and unstructured data for comprehensive analysis is complex.

Strategies for Managing Data Variety

- **Data Lakes:** Centralized repositories for storing both structured and unstructured data.
- **NoSQL Databases:** Handling unstructured and semi-structured data with flexibility.

- **Data Integration Tools:** Combining data from different sources into a unified view.
- **Data Enrichment:** Adding context to unstructured data for better analysis.
- **Text Analytics:** Extracting information from unstructured text data.
- **Machine Learning:** Applying algorithms to uncover patterns in both structured and unstructured data.

By effectively managing data variety, organizations can unlock valuable insights and gain a competitive advantage.

Data Velocity:

Data velocity refers to the speed at which data is generated and processed. It's about capturing, processing, and analyzing data as it arrives, rather than in batches. This is crucial for industries like finance, telecommunications, and e-commerce, where timely insights drive business decisions.

Challenges of High-Velocity Data

Data Ingestion:

Data ingestion is the critical first step in the data pipeline, involving capturing and storing incoming data efficiently. Given the increasing volume and velocity of data, this process has become increasingly complex.

Key Challenges in Data Ingestion

- **Data Volume:** Handling massive amounts of data in real-time.
- **Data Velocity:** Processing data as it arrives, with low latency.
- **Data Variety:** Dealing with structured, unstructured, and semi-structured data.
- **Data Quality:** Ensuring data accuracy, completeness, and consistency.

Strategies for Efficient Data Ingestion

- **Real-Time Processing:** Using technologies like Apache Kafka, Apache Flink, or Kinesis to handle high-velocity data streams.
- **Batch Processing:** For less time-sensitive data, using tools like Hadoop or Spark for bulk data loading.
- **Data Validation:** Implementing data quality checks at the ingestion point to ensure data integrity.
- **Data Transformation:** Converting data into a suitable format for storage and processing.
- **Data Storage:** Selecting appropriate storage solutions (HDFS, object storage, data lakes) based on data volume, variety, and access patterns.
- **Error Handling:** Implementing mechanisms to handle data ingestion failures and retries.

Popular Data Ingestion Tools

- **Apache Kafka:** A distributed streaming platform for handling high-throughput data feeds.
- **Apache Flume:** A distributed, reliable, and available system for collecting, aggregating, and moving large amounts of log data.
- **Apache Sqoop:** For transferring data between Hadoop and relational databases.
- **AWS Kinesis:** A fully managed service for real-time processing of streaming data.
- **Azure Event Hubs:** A fully managed capture and store service for big data.
- **Google Cloud Pub/Sub:** A fully managed real-time messaging service.

Best Practices for Data Ingestion

- **Data Profiling:** Understanding data characteristics before ingestion.
- **Data Partitioning:** Dividing data into smaller, manageable chunks.

- **Data Compression:** Reducing data size to optimize storage and processing.
- **Load Balancing:** Distributing incoming data across multiple nodes.
- **Error Handling and Retries:** Implementing mechanisms to handle failures and ensure data reliability.

By implementing these strategies and leveraging appropriate tools, organizations can efficiently capture and store rapidly incoming data, laying the foundation for valuable insights and decision-making.

Data Processing:

Data processing in real-time or near real-time involves transforming raw data into meaningful insights as soon as it's generated. This capability is crucial for industries like finance, e-commerce, and IoT, where timely decisions are essential.

Key Challenges in Real-Time Processing

- **Data Volume:** Handling massive amounts of incoming data.
- **Data Velocity:** Processing data with minimal latency.
- **Data Variety:** Dealing with diverse data types (structured, unstructured, semi-structured).
- **Complexity:** Performing complex calculations and analyses on the fly.

Technologies for Real-Time Processing

- **Stream Processing Platforms:** Apache Kafka, Apache Flink, Apache Storm for handling high-velocity data streams.
- **In-Memory Databases:** For fast data access and processing.
- **Complex Event Processing (CEP):** For detecting patterns and events in real-time data streams.
- **Machine Learning:** Applying ML algorithms on streaming data for real-time predictions.

Use Cases for Real-Time Processing

- **Fraud Detection:** Identifying suspicious activities in real-time.
- **Customer Analytics:** Analyzing customer behavior for personalized recommendations.
- **IoT Applications:** Monitoring and analyzing sensor data for predictive maintenance.
- **Financial Trading:** Making rapid trading decisions based on market data.

Best Practices for Real-Time Processing

- **Data Validation:** Ensuring data quality before processing.
- **Incremental Updates:** Processing data in batches for efficiency while maintaining near real-time insights.
- **Error Handling:** Implementing robust error handling mechanisms.
- **Performance Optimization:** Continuously monitoring and optimizing processing performance.

By effectively addressing these challenges and leveraging appropriate technologies, organizations can unlock the full potential of their data through real-time insights.

Latency:

Latency refers to the time delay between data generation and the moment it becomes available for consumption and analysis. In today's data-driven world, minimizing latency is crucial for making timely decisions and gaining a competitive edge.

Factors Affecting Latency

- **Network Latency:** Delays in data transmission over networks.
- **Data Processing Latency:** Time taken to transform raw data into usable information.
- **Storage Latency:** Time taken to read or write data from storage.
- **Query Latency:** Time taken to execute queries on the data.

- **Application Latency:** Delays in data processing and presentation within applications.

Minimizing Latency

- **Real-time Processing**: Employing technologies like Apache Kafka, Apache Flink, and Apache Storm for low-latency data processing.
- **In-MemoryComputing**: Utilizing in-memory databases for faster data access and processing.
- **Edge Computing**: Processing data closer to the data source to reduce network latency.
- **Caching**: Storing frequently accessed data in memory for faster retrieval.
- **Compression**: Reducing data size to improve transmission and processing speeds.
- **Optimized Data Structures**: Using data structures that support efficient access and manipulation.
- **Parallel Processing**: Distributing processing tasks across multiple nodes.

Challenges and Considerations

- **Trade-offs:** Often, there's a trade-off between latency and cost.
- **Data Volume:** High data volumes can increase latency.
- **Data Complexity:** Complex data transformations can add to latency.
- **Network Congestion:** Network traffic can impact latency.

By carefully considering these factors and implementing appropriate strategies, organizations can significantly reduce latency and gain a competitive advantage.

Scalability:

Scalability is the ability of a system to handle increasing workloads or data volumes without compromising performance or requiring significant architectural changes. In the realm of data management, this means ensuring your infrastructure can handle growing datasets and processing demands.

Key Scaling Strategies

- **Horizontal Scaling**: Adding more nodes to a cluster to distribute the workload. This is often the preferred approach for big data systems.
- **Vertical Scaling**: Increasing the resources (CPU, memory, storage) of existing nodes. This is limited by hardware constraints.
- **Sharding**: Partitioning data across multiple nodes based on specific criteria.
- **Data Replication**: Creating copies of data across multiple nodes for redundancy and improved performance.
- **Load Balancing**: Distributing incoming traffic across multiple servers to prevent bottlenecks.

Challenges in Scaling

- **Data Distribution**: Ensuring data is evenly distributed across nodes for optimal performance.
- **Data Consistency**: Maintaining data consistency across multiple nodes.
- **Network Latency**: Managing increased network traffic and latency.
- **Cost:** Balancing scalability with cost-effectiveness.
- **Complexity**: Managing a distributed system can be complex.

Examples of Scalable Systems

- **Hadoop Distributed File System (HDFS)**: Designed for storing and processing massive datasets across clusters of computers.
- **NoSQL databases**: Offer horizontal scalability to handle increasing data volumes.

- **Cloud-based platforms**: Provide elastic scalability with pay-as-you-go pricing models.

Best Practices for Scalability

Start Small:

The principle of "start small" is fundamental in data management and analytics. By initiating with a manageable system, organizations can:

Benefits of Starting Small

- **Reduced Costs**: Lower initial investment in hardware, software, and personnel.
- **Faster Time to Market**: Quicker deployment and value realization.
- **Risk Mitigation**: Lower risk of significant financial loss or data breaches.
- **Focused Development**: Prioritize core functionalities and iterate based on feedback.
- **Proof of Concept**: Validate the solution's viability before full-scale implementation.

Key Considerations

- **Scalability:** Ensure the chosen system can handle future growth.
- **Flexibility:** Select tools and technologies that can adapt to changing requirements.
- **Modularity:** Design the system with loosely coupled components for easier expansion.
- **Monitoring:** Implement robust monitoring to track system performance and identify bottlenecks.
- **Iteration:** Continuously evaluate and refine the system based on feedback and insights.

Examples of Starting Small

- **Data Warehousing**: Begin with a subset of data and gradually expand the data warehouse.
- **Cloud-Based Solutions**: Leverage pay-as-you-go models to scale resources based on demand.
- **Pilot Projects**: Implement a small-scale project to test data management and analytics capabilities.

By adopting a "start small" approach, organizations can lay a solid foundation for their data initiatives, minimize risks, and achieve long-term success.

Modular Design:

Modular design is a cornerstone of scalable systems. By breaking down a complex system into smaller, independent components, organizations can enhance flexibility, maintainability, and scalability.

Key Principles of Modular Design

- **Loose Coupling**: Components should interact with minimal dependencies, allowing for independent changes.
- **High Cohesion**: Each component should have a well-defined purpose and functionality.
- **Encapsulation**: Components should hide internal details and expose only necessary interfaces.
- **Standardization**: Use consistent interfaces and data formats for seamless integration.
- **Reusability**: Design components to be reusable in different contexts.

Benefits of Modular Design

- **Scalability**: Independent components can be scaled independently based on demand.
- **Maintainability**: Easier to isolate and fix issues within specific modules.

- **Reusability**: Reduces development time and effort by leveraging existing components.
- **Flexibility**: Adaptability to changing requirements through modular updates.
- **Testability**: Improved testing capabilities due to isolated components.

Examples of Modular Design in Data Management

- **DataPipeline**: Breaking down the data pipeline into stages (extraction, transformation, loading) with independent components.
- **MicroservicesArchitecture**: Building data processing applications as a collection of loosely coupled services.
- **DataLakeArchitecture**: Organizing data into zones (landing, curated, processed) with clear boundaries.

Challenges and Considerations

- **IncreasedComplexity**: Managing multiple components can introduce overhead.
- **Interdependencies**: Careful design is required to avoid unintended consequences.
- **DataConsistency**: Ensuring data consistency across modules can be challenging.

By adopting modular design principles, organizations can create scalable and maintainable data management systems that can adapt to evolving business needs.

Performance Monitoring:

Performance monitoring is the continuous observation and measurement of system performance to identify potential bottlenecks, optimize resource utilization, and ensure optimal system health.

Key Metrics to Monitor

- **Resource Utilization**: CPU, memory, disk I/O, network bandwidth
- **Response Time**: Time taken for the system to respond to requests
- **Throughput**: The number of transactions or requests processed per unit of time
- **Error Rates**: Frequency of system failures or errors
- **Latency**: Time taken for data to travel between system components

Tools and Technologies

- **Infrastructure Monitoring Tools:** Zabbix, Nagios, Prometheus
- **Application Performance Monitoring (APM):** New Relic, Dynatrace, AppDynamics
- **Log Management:** Splunk, ELK Stack
- **Cloud-Based Monitoring: AWS** CloudWatch, Azure Monitor, Google Cloud Monitoring

Identifying Bottlenecks

- **CorrelationAnalysis**: Identifying relationships between metrics to pinpoint root causes.
- **Baselining**: Establishing normal performance levels for comparison.
- **AnomalyDetection**: Identifying unusual patterns or spikes in metrics.
- **Profiling**: Analyzing code execution to identify performance hotspots.

Best Practices

- **Establish Clear Service Level Objectives (SLOs):** Define performance expectations.

- **ImplementAlerting**: Set up notifications for critical performance issues.
- **ContinuousOptimization**: Regularly analyze performance data and make improvements.
- **RootCauseAnalysis**: Investigate the underlying causes of performance problems.
- **CapacityPlanning**: Forecast future resource needs based on performance data.

By effectively monitoring system performance and identifying bottlenecks, organizations can optimize resource utilization, improve user experience, and prevent system failures.

Capacity Planning:

Capacity planning is the process of determining the production capacity needed to meet future demand. It involves analyzing business resources, identifying potential bottlenecks, and assessing resource utilization.

Key Components of Capacity Planning

- **DemandForecasting**: Predicting future demand based on historical data, market trends, and external factors.
- **ResourceAssessment**: Evaluating existing resources (people, equipment, technology) and their capacity.
- **CapacityGapAnalysis**: Identifying the difference between projected demand and available capacity.
- **CapacityExpansion**: Developing strategies to increase capacity, such as adding resources, improving efficiency, or outsourcing.
- **RiskAssessment**: Identifying potential risks and developing contingency plans.

Capacity Planning Techniques

- **Top-DownApproach**: Starts with overall business objectives and translates them into capacity requirements.

- **Bottom-UpApproach**: Begins with individual departments or processes and aggregates their capacity needs.
- **SimulationModeling**: Creating virtual models to simulate different scenarios and assess capacity requirements.

Challenges in Capacity Planning

- **DemandUncertainty**: Predicting future demand accurately can be challenging.
- **ResourceConstraints:** Limited availability of resources (financial, human, technological).
- **EconomicConditions:** External factors impacting business operations.
- **TechnologicalAdvancements:** Rapid changes in technology affecting capacity needs.

Best Practices

- **ContinuousMonitoring**: Regularly assess capacity utilization and adjust plans as needed.
- **Collaboration**: Involve stakeholders from different departments in the planning process.
- **Flexibility**: Build in flexibility to adapt to changing circumstances.
- **RiskManagement**: Identify potential risks and develop mitigation strategies.

By effectively implementing capacity planning, organizations can avoid over- or under-investment in resources, optimize operations, and ensure they are well-positioned for future growth.

Load Testing:

Load testing is a critical component of ensuring system reliability and performance. It involves simulating real-world user loads to assess how a system behaves under expected and peak conditions.

Key Objectives of Load Testing

- **IdentifyPerformanceBottlenecks**: Pinpoint areas where the system struggles under load.
- **MeasureResponseTimes**: Evaluate how quickly the system responds to user requests.
- **DetermineScalability**: Assess the system's ability to handle increasing user loads.
- **ValidatePerformance Metrics:** Ensure the system meets performance requirements.

Load Testing Process

- **Define Test Scenarios**: Identify typical user behaviors and create representative test scripts.
- **Design Test Environment**: Set up a testing environment that mimics the production environment.
- **Generate Load**: Simulate user traffic using load testing tools to create desired load conditions.
- **Monitor Performance**: Collect performance metrics such as response times, throughput, and error rates.
- **Analyze Results**: Identify performance bottlenecks and areas for improvement.

Load Testing Tools

- **Open-source tools**: Apache JMeter, Locust
- **Commercial tools**: LoadRunner, Gatling, BlazeMeter

Types of Load Tests

- **Volume Testing**: Simulates a large number of users accessing the system simultaneously.
- **Stress Testing**: Exceeds normal load to determine the system's breaking point.

- **Endurance Testing**: Simulates sustained load over an extended period to assess system stability.
- **Spike Testing**: Simulates sudden bursts of traffic to evaluate system responsiveness.

Best Practices

- **Realistic Load Scenarios**: Create test scenarios that accurately reflect real-world usage patterns.
- **Monitoring Key Metrics**: Track relevant performance metrics to identify issues.
- **Iterative Testing**: Conduct multiple test iterations to refine the system.
- **Correlation Analysis**: Identify dependencies between system components.
- **Continuous Load Testing**: Incorporate load testing into the development lifecycle.

By conducting thorough load testing, organizations can identify performance issues early in the development process, optimize system performance, and deliver a high-quality user experience. By carefully considering these factors and implementing appropriate strategies, organizations can build scalable data management systems that can handle growing data volumes and processing demands while maintaining performance and efficiency.

Technologies for Handling High-Velocity Data

Stream Processing:

Stream processing platforms are the cornerstone of real-time data processing, enabling organizations to extract immediate value from rapidly incoming data streams.

Key Platforms

- **Apache Kafka**: Primarily a distributed event streaming platform, it excels at ingesting and distributing high-volume data streams. Kafka can also be used for simple stream processing tasks through Kafka Streams.

- **Apache Flink**: A versatile stream processing framework offering both batch and stream processing capabilities. It supports stateful computations, making it suitable for complex real-time applications.
- **Apache Storm**: Known for its high performance and fault tolerance, Storm is well-suited for real-time analytics and distributed computing.

Core Components and Functionalities

- **Data Ingestion**: Efficiently capturing data from various sources (IoT devices, web applications, databases).
- **Data Transformation**: Processing and enriching data to extract meaningful information.
- **Data Aggregation**: Combining data from multiple streams for analysis.
- **StateManagement**: Storing intermediate results for complex calculations and stateful computations.
- **Windowing**: Grouping data into time-based windows for analysis.
- **Error Handling**: Ensuring data integrity and reliability.

Challenges and Considerations

- **Data Volume and Velocity**: Handling high-throughput data streams efficiently.
- **Latency**: Minimizing delays in data processing and analysis.
- **State Management**: Managing stateful computations without compromising performance.
- **Fault Tolerance**: Ensuring system reliability in case of failures.
- **Scalability**: Adapting to increasing data volumes and processing demands.

Use Cases

- **Fraud Detection**: Identifying suspicious activities in real-time.
- **IoT Analytics**: Processing sensor data for predictive maintenance.
- **Customer Analytics**: Analyzing customer behavior for personalized recommendations.
- **Financial Trading**: Making rapid trading decisions based on market data.
- **Real-timeRecommendations**: Providing personalized product recommendations.

By understanding the capabilities of these platforms and addressing the challenges, organizations can effectively leverage stream processing to gain competitive advantages through real-time insights.

In-Memory Computing:

- In-memory computing involves storing and processing data directly in a computer's main memory (RAM) rather than on slower storage devices like hard drives.
- This approach dramatically accelerates data processing speeds, enabling real-time analytics and interactive data exploration.

Key Benefits of In-Memory Computing

- **Speed**: Dramatically faster data processing compared to disk-based systems.
- **IterativeAlgorithms**: Efficiently executing iterative algorithms like machine learning models.
- **InteractiveAnalysis**: Enabling real-time exploration and visualization of data.
- **LowLatency**: Minimizing response times for critical applications.

Apache Spark:

Apache Spark is a powerful and versatile framework that excels in in-memory computing. It offers several key advantages:

- **UnifiedEngine**: Supports batch, streaming, SQL, machine learning, and graph processing workloads.
- **FaultTolerance**: Ensures data reliability through checkpointing and recovery mechanisms.
- **Scalability**: Handles large datasets and complex computations efficiently.
- **RichEcosystem**: Integrates with various data sources and tools.

Challenges and Considerations

- **MemoryConstraints**: Limited RAM capacity can restrict the amount of data that can be processed in-memory.
- **DataVolume**: Handling extremely large datasets might require hybrid approaches combining in-memory and disk-based storage.
- **Cost**: In-memory computing can be more expensive due to higher hardware costs.
- **DataLoss**: Risk of data loss in case of system failures if not properly managed.

Use Cases

- **Real-timeAnalytics**: Processing streaming data for immediate insights.
- **InteractiveDataExploration**: Enabling users to explore data interactively.
- **MachineLearning**: Accelerating model training and inference.
- **RiskManagement**: Real-time fraud detection and risk assessment.

By effectively leveraging in-memory computing technologies like Apache Spark, organizations can gain significant performance improvements and unlock new possibilities for data-driven decision-making.

Time-Series Databases:

Time-series databases are specifically designed to handle and query data that changes over time.

Key Characteristics of Time-Series Databases

- **High Ingestion Rates**: Can handle massive volumes of data points per second.
- **Efficient Storage**: Optimized for storing large amounts of time-stamped data.
- **Fast Querying**: Support for complex queries on time-series data, including aggregations, filtering, and downsampling.
- **Data Compression**: Employ compression techniques to reduce storage requirements.
- **Time-Based Indexing**: Indexes are optimized for time-based access patterns.

Popular Time-Series Databases

- **InfluxDB:** Open-source platform with a focus on time-series metrics.
- **TimescaleDB:** Extends PostgreSQL with time-series capabilities.
- **Prometheus:** Primarily used for monitoring and alerting, but also offers time-series capabilities.
- **ClickHouse:** Known for its high performance and analytical capabilities.

Common Use Cases

- **IoTSensorData**: Storing and analyzing data from connected devices.
- **FinancialData**: Tracking stock prices, market trends, and trading activities.

- **Telecommunications**: Monitoring network performance and usage.
- **ITMonitoring**: Tracking system metrics and performance.

Challenges and Considerations

- **DataVolume**: Handling massive amounts of time-series data efficiently.
- **DataRetention**: Determining appropriate data retention policies.
- **DataQuality**: Ensuring data accuracy and consistency.
- **QueryPerformance**: Optimizing query performance for various use cases.

By understanding the characteristics and capabilities of time-series databases, organizations can effectively manage and derive insights from their time-stamped data.

NoSQL Databases:

NoSQL databases are designed to handle the challenges posed by unstructured and semi-structured data, which are increasingly prevalent in today's data-driven world. These databases offer flexibility, scalability, and high performance, making them ideal for a wide range of applications.

Key Characteristics of NoSQL Databases

- **FlexibleSchema**: Accommodates diverse data structures without rigid schemas.
- **Scalability**: Handles massive amounts of data by distributing it across multiple nodes.
- **HighPerformance**: Optimized for rapid read and write operations.
- **FaultTolerance**: Ensures data availability through replication and redundancy.

Types of NoSQL Databases

- **DocumentDatabases:** Store data in flexible, JSON-like documents (MongoDB, Couchbase).
- **Key-ValueStores:** Simple data structures with key-value pairs (Redis, Amazon DynamoDB).
- **Wide-ColumnStores:** Organize data into columns, allowing flexible schema (Cassandra, HBase).
- **GraphDatabases:** Represent data as nodes and relationships (Neo4j, Amazon Neptune).

Use Cases for NoSQL Databases

- **ContentManagementSystems:** Storing rich media, blogs, and articles.
- **Real-timeAnalytics:** Processing and analyzing large volumes of unstructured data.
- **MobileandIoTApplications:** Handling diverse data structures and high-velocity data streams.
- **SocialMedia:** Managing user profiles, posts, and relationships.
- **E-commerce:** Storing product catalogs, customer data, and order information.

Challenges and Considerations

- **Data Modeling:** Designing appropriate data structures for unstructured data.
- **Query Complexity:** Complex queries might be challenging compared to SQL databases.
- **Data Consistency:** Ensuring data consistency across distributed systems.
- **Data Integration:** Integrating NoSQL with other data sources.

By carefully selecting the appropriate NoSQL database and addressing these challenges, organizations can effectively manage unstructured and semi-structured data, unlocking valuable insights and driving innovation.

Use Cases for Real-Time Analytics

- **Fraud Detection:** Identifying suspicious activities in real-time.
- **Customer Insights:**Analyzing customer behavior for personalized recommendations.
- **IoT Applications:** Processing data from connected devices for predictive maintenance.
- **Financial Trading:** Making rapid trading decisions based on market data.

By effectively managing data velocity, organizations can gain a competitive edge by making timely and informed decisions. Despite these challenges, big data analytics offers immense opportunities for business analysts to become strategic partners in driving business growth and innovation.

CHAPTER ELEVEN

CONCLUSION

Big data analytics is no longer a luxury but a necessity for organizations seeking a competitive edge. It empowers businesses to transform raw data into actionable insights that drive growth, innovation, and efficiency. By understanding the core concepts, mastering essential tools and techniques, and addressing the inherent challenges, organizations can unlock the full potential of their data.

From the vast landscape of data, we've explored how to navigate its complexities. We've delved into the roles of data scientists and business analysts, understanding their unique contributions to the big data ecosystem. We've also highlighted the importance of ethical considerations and the evolving nature of the field.

The journey to mastering big data analytics is continuous. As technology advances and data volumes explode, the ability to extract value will become increasingly critical. By staying updated on emerging trends and best practices, organizations can position themselves at the forefront of data-driven innovation.

Ultimately, the successful implementation of big data analytics requires a strategic approach that combines technological expertise with a deep understanding of business objectives. By aligning data initiatives with organizational goals, businesses can harness the power of big data to create a sustainable competitive advantage.

CHAPTER TWELVE

REFERENCES

1. B.Thillaieswari., "Comparative Study on Tools and Techniques of Big Data Analysis" International Journal of Advanced Networking & Applications (IJANA) Volume: 08, Issue: 05 Pages: 61-66 (2017) Special Issue.
2. Elgendy,N. "Big Data Analytics in Support of the Decision Making Process", MSc Thesis, German University in Cairo, p. 164 (2013).
3. Kaisler S, Armour F, Espinosa JA, Money W. "Big data: issues and challenges moving forward" In: System sciences (HICSS), 2013 46th Hawaii international conference on, IEEE. 2013. pp. 995–1004.
4. Kubick, W.R. "Big Data, Information and Meaning", In: Clinical Trial Insights, pp. 26–28 (2012)
5. Khan N, Yaqoob I, Hashem IAT, et al. "Big data: survey, technologies, opportunities, and challenges", Sci World J. 2014;2014:712826.
6. TechAmerica: "Demystifying Big Data: A Practical Guide to Transforming the Business of Government", In: TechAmerica Reports, pp. 1–40 (2012)
7. Manyika, J., Chui, M., Brown, B., Bughin, J., Dobbs, R., Roxburgh, C., Byers, A.H.,"Big Data: The Next Frontier for Innovation, Competition, and Productivity", In: McKinsey Global Institute Reports, pp. 1–156 (2011)

8. Russom, P, "Big Data Analytics. In: TDWI Best Practices Report", pp. 1–40 (2011).
9. Song, Z., Kusiak, A, "Optimizing Product Configurations with a Data Mining Approach", International Journal of Production Research 47(7), 1733–1751 (2009).
10. Thuan L. Nguyen , "A Framework for Five Big V's of Big Data and Organizational Culture in Firms", IEEE International Conference on big Data Mining Workshops ,pp 5411-5413(2018).
11. Ms. Komal , "A Review Paper on Big Data Analytics Tools" (IJTIMES), e-ISSN: 2455-2585 Volume 4, Issue 5, May-2018, pp 1012-1017.
12. Nirmal Kaur, Gurpinder Singh, "A Review Paper On Data Mining And Big Data", International Journal of Advanced Research in Computer Science, Volume 8, No. 4, May 2017, ISSN No 076-567, pp 407-409.
13. J.Nageswara Rao, M.Ramesh, "A Review on Data Mining & Big Data, Machine Learning Techniques" , International Journal of Recent Technology and Engineering (IJRTE) ISSN: 2277-3878, Volume-7 Issue-6S2, April 2019, pp 914-916.
14. E.Kuiler.From Big Data to Knowledge: An Ontological Approach to Big Data Analytics, Review of Policy Research, Vol.31, No.4 (2014).
15. A.Konys, W. Rogoza. Big Data and Ontologies. Talk at ACS Int. Conf. 2016 in Miedzyzdroje, Oct. 2016, 3p.
16. B. Marr, J. Wiley. Big Data: Using SMART Big Data, Analytics and Metrics to Make Better Decisions and Improve Performance, Sons Ltd, 2015.
17. L.Globa, I. Svetsynska, A. Luntovskyy. Case Studies on Big Data, Journal of Theoretical and Applied Computer Science, JTACS, Polish Academy of Science, Gdansk, No. 2, 2016, ISSN 2299-2634.

www.ingramcontent.com/pod-product-compliance
Lightning Source LLC
LaVergne TN
LVHW021140160826
845679LV00023B/1983

9798895196724